Women Redefining Leadership with S.P.I.C.E.®

A Bold New Vision for Modern Leadership

Visionary Author: Shayla N. Atkins

Featuring Trailblazing Women Executives, CEOs, and Visionary Leaders

Copyright 2025. Shayla N. Atkins, The Atkins Impact

All rights reserved. No part of this publication may be reproduced, distributed, or transmitted in any form or by any means, including photocopying, recording, or other electronic or mechanical methods, without the prior written permission of the original author, except in the case of brief quotations embedded in critical articles, reviews, and certain other noncommercial uses permitted by copyright law.

Paperback ISBN: 979-8-218-61498-0
Hardcover ISBN: 979-8-218-61499-7
Electronic Kindle ISBN: 979-8-9926778-0-5
Corporate Edition Paperback ISBN: 979-8-218-61500-0

Table of Contents

Foreword   5
    by DeRetta Rhodes, PhD
Preface   8

Chapter 1: Introverts Leading with S.P.I.C.E.   10
    From Surviving in the Shadows to Thriving Authentically
    About the Author: Shayla N. Atkins, PHR, LSSBB   33

Part 1: Business SAVVY   36
    The Power of Strategic Leadership

Chapter 2: Breaking the Mold in a Male Dominated World   37
    Lessons in Redefining Leadership
    About the Author: Melissa Mack   54

Chapter 3: The Savvy Culture Leader   57
    Balancing Heart and Head for Transformational Impact
    About the Author: Mildred Black   72

Part 2: Strategic PERFORMANCE   75
    Elevating Impact Without Burnout

Chapter 4: Owning Your Performance Narrative   76
    Your Work Speaks for Itself – Make Sure It's Heard
    About the Author: Kristin Bell, SPHR   94

Chapter 5: Redefining Executive Leadership Through Health and Wellbeing   97
    Being Healthy and Successful Looks Good on You
    About the Author: Dr. Alicia Newsome   118

Chapter 6: The Journey & Lessons to Achieving Optimal Performance   121
    Harnessing P.E.A.K. Purpose and Resilience to Overcome Adversity
    About to Author: Patrice Key   139

Part 3: Authentic IMAGE   142
    Authentic Personal Brand, Influence & Credibility

Chapter 7: Becoming Chakla, Leading Boldly, Living Unapologetically — 143
    Embracing Purpose, Courage, and Authenticity to Inspire Others
    About the Author: Chakla Davis — 157

Chapter 8: The Expert In The Room — 160
    Defining Leadership Beyond Age, Gender and Stereotypes
    About the Author: Que Parnell, PharmD — 175

Chapter 9: Unapologetically Visible — 178
    Redefining Professional Image for Black Women
    About the Author: Shaunda Thompson — 202

Part 4: Compelling COMMUNICATION — 205
    The Art of Influence & Advocacy

Chapter 10: Authentic Advocacy in Action — 206
    Owning Your Voice and Vision
    About the Author: Juwayriyah Hussain — 225

Chapter 11: Strengthen Your Network — 228
    Gaining Exposure Through Communication
    About the Author: Terri Barnes — 248

Part 5: Intentional EXPOSURE — 250
    Intentionally Positioning Yourself for Opportunities

Chapter 12: Thrusted Into Leadership — 251
    From Uncertain Teen to International Influence
    About the Author: Dr. Tabatha Russell — 266

Chapter 13: Intentional Exposure — 269
    Embrace Your Wait; Timing Is Everything...
    About the Author: Stephanie Johnson — 285

CONCLUSION: The Call to Redefine Leadership; Together — 287
    Shayla N. Atkins

Foreword

There are times in your life when you have a magnanimous opportunity. As I write about this extraordinary book, Women Redefining Leadership with S.P.I.C.E. – A Bold New Vision for Modern Leadership, I feel privileged to introduce you to a work that will inspire, empower, and challenge you to redefine leadership in your life and career. This book is a jewel, a beacon for women who have achieved or aspire to senior leadership roles across any sector.

This book allows you to validate your identity, amplify your voice, gain recognition, and ensure you are illuminating your personal brand in intentional and impactful ways. The brilliant authors of the chapters that comprise this book provide you with actionable insights on harmonizing effectiveness, strategy, wellness, and influence to ascend in many levels of your life, both professionally and personally.

Each author shares their journey with transparency and vulnerability, making their stories deeply relatable. Their experiences are more than narrative; they are compasses, pointing readers toward actionable strategies for your leadership development as you grow in your self-leadership. Each author delves into critical areas of career success: savvy, performance, image, communication, and exposure, coined as S.P.I.C.E., by sharing their personal stories, challenges, successes, and triumphs which have made each of them a game changer in their respective fields and expertise. You'll hear from leaders who have navigated adversity, shattered ceilings, and redefined success on their terms. Their journeys are a testament to the power of resilience, courage, and individuality in leadership.

The timing of this book is profound. In an era where leadership needs to be reimagined, this work provides timeless wisdom, offering inspiration to many and guidance to women and men in leadership. What makes this book truly exceptional is its focus on authenticity. It highlights the critical need to lead with purpose, emotional intelligence, resilience, wellness, and empathy, providing tools that resonate not only for women but for anyone committed to redefining leadership. You will find that it provides an expansive approach that can be applied in every medium imaginable, development programs, executive retreats, leadership conferences, and beyond.

Women Redefining Leadership with S.P.I.C.E. is needed now more than ever as it provides a fresh and innovative way to approach leadership that has often used outdated and century-old approaches that do not include the diversity and inclusion that is so critically needed in these times, especially for women of color. It provides a provocative approach that provides a new leadership playbook that all should use. It gives approaches to women by women; and all.

It has been a pleasure and a treat to meet each of the women and hear their stories. You will want to share in their experiences!

Preface

Why Redefining Leadership?

Leadership, as we have traditionally understood it, is at a crossroads. Today's leadership standards, rooted in principles nearly a century old, can no longer meet the demands of an increasingly complex, diverse, and volatile business environment. Since 1920, leadership has deprioritized skills such as empathy, emotional intelligence, inclusion, and authenticity by labeling them as "soft skills." Yet, these are the very qualities essential for effectively leading people, teams…humans. These traits can, and should, become the new norm. Poor leadership practices cost American companies an estimated $630 billion annually due to decreased productivity, turnover, and disengagement.

It is clear: the time for change is now.

Women, in particular, face significant barriers in leadership. Despite comprising nearly half the workforce, women hold only 25% of senior leadership positions in the United States. The numbers are even more stark for women of color: Black and Latina women together hold less than 5% of senior leadership roles. Additionally, over 40% of women executive's report feeling burned out, a reflection of the increased stress and overperformance required to succeed in environments that often overlook or undervalue their contributions.

This book, *Women Redefining Leadership With S.P.I.C.E. – A Bold New Vision for Modern Leadership,* is a call to action. It is a movement to redefine leadership standards and employee experiences by cultivating and advancing authentic, inclusive, and strategic leaders who drive exceptional outcomes for both people and business. This anthology brings together the voices of trailblazing women CEOs, corporate leaders, and change-makers who are leading the charge, have navigated challenges and seized opportunities to create lasting impact. Their stories are filled with hard-won wisdom, actionable insights, and the raw truth about the realities of leadership.

This book is more than a collection of stories. It is a guide for leaders who are ready to rise to the challenges of a rapidly evolving world. The leaders featured in this anthology are at the forefront of this transformation, redefining leadership through authenticity, emotional intelligence, and empathy while excelling in strategic impact and delivering exceptional business outcomes. Their contributions are not just a response to the challenges of today's workplace; they are a blueprint for the future.

Let these stories guide you, inspire you, and remind you that leadership is not static; it is dynamic, transformative, and deeply personal. Each chapter offers actionable insights, practical tools, and strategies to help you navigate your own leadership journey with confidence and clarity.

Welcome to *Women Redefining Leadership With S.P.I.C.E. – A Bold New Vision for Modern Leadership.*

Chapter 1

Introverts Leading with S.P.I.C.E.®

From Surviving in the Shadows to Thriving Authentically

Shayla N. Atkins

Introduction

Leadership is often characterized by bold voices, extroverted personas, and outward charisma. Yet, as a significant portion of the population, introverts possess a different but equally powerful style of leadership. For many, the experience of leadership is deeply personal, shaped by early lessons, societal norms, and personal temperament. As a natural introvert, my early encounters with leadership were framed by well-meaning but limiting advice: "keep your head down," "don't ruffle feathers", "do a good job and you'll get noticed". These mantras seemed to align with my natural disposition, reinforcing the idea that visibility and self-promotion were unnecessary or even undesirable.

For years, I believed that my quiet diligence and unwavering focus were enough. My work would garner recognition on its own, and opportunities would naturally follow. However, as I navigated the complexities of the corporate world, I realized that this approach often left me overlooked. My ideas were brilliant but unclaimed, and often times no longer my ideas. My contributions were impactful but credited to others. While I excelled at executing and strategizing, I was operating in the shadows, far from the recognition and influence I aspired to achieve.

This chapter explores how introverts can excel as leaders by leveraging their innate strengths through the S.P.I.C.E. framework: Savvy, Performance, Image, Communication, and Exposure. But more than a framework, this is an invitation to rethink how we identify top talent. Introverts bring unique qualities to the table, deep thinking, emotional intelligence, and purposeful action that, when harnessed, can redefine leadership itself. My journey of moving from a silent contributor to an intentional, visible leader is a testament to the power of leaning into one's introverted nature, rather than fighting against it.

Leading In The Shadows

Growing up, I was taught to "keep my head down," "let your work speak for itself," and "be seen, not heard." These mantras weren't just guidelines; they were rules, etched into my approach to life and work. At my first job, I was the epitome of diligence. I clocked in early, worked tirelessly, and avoided unnecessary interactions. My natural introversion made these principles feel not just comfortable, but right.

At the time, I believed wholeheartedly in the notion that excellence would naturally be rewarded. I convinced myself that being invisible, except for the quality of my work, was a strength. But as I climbed the ladder of my career, the cracks in this belief began to show. I watched as others, sometimes less qualified, less dedicated, stepped forward boldly, claiming the credit and reaping the rewards for work that was often mine.

I told myself it was okay. After all, I didn't need the spotlight. Yet, a part of me felt the sting of invisibility, the frustration of being overlooked. I was delivering brilliance in the shadows, but my career started stagnating. Promotions were sporadic, recognition fleeting, and my professional path felt more like a series of happenstances than a carefully crafted journey. My introversion, once comforting, now felt like a weight holding me back. I had an unwavering desire to succeed, so I decided to take action and step out of the shadows.

Breaking The Mold, Or So I Thought

This drive to succeed, however, was not just fueled by ambition but by a belief that I needed to emulate the leadership styles I saw rewarded in my organization. I adopted a more extroverted, masculine approach to leadership, commanding, controlling, and conforming, because I believed that was the path to promotion and recognition.

At first, this strategy seemed to work. I was noticed, promoted, and even praised for my ability to take charge. But the cost was staggering. In striving to mold myself into an identity that wasn't mine, I became a perfectionist, constantly chasing an impossible standard. My every decision and action felt like a performance, and the weight of maintaining this facade was overwhelming. While outwardly successful, I felt deeply conflicted and hollow inside.

As the demands grew, I pushed myself harder, often working late into the night and ignoring my own well-being.

Exhaustion became my baseline, but I told myself it was the price of success. I rationalized the physical toll, the headaches, sleepless nights, the fertility challenges and unrelenting stress, as temporary sacrifices, you know greatness comes at a cost. Until one day, my body had enough. I found myself hospitalized and physically and emotionally depleted. It was as if my body had called a timeout, forcing me to confront what I had long avoided: the way I had been operating was not just unsustainable, it was destructive.

As I lay in that hospital bed, the beeping of monitors and sterile white walls became a backdrop for reflection. I realized that the way I had been living, pushing, striving, hiding, wasn't just draining me; it was diminishing me. I had poured so much into proving my worth through silent, unnoticed brilliance that I had nothing left to give.

The Turning Point

The road to clarity often requires us to reach a breaking point, and for me, that moment came with a profound realization after years of pushing myself to fit into molds that weren't mine. My body had already sent its warning signals, and the health scare had made it impossible to ignore the toll my choices had taken on me. I slowed down, began to take care of myself and I experienced a miracle, the moment when everything came into focus, was deeply personal and life-altering: the birth of my twin daughters.

Their arrival was a revelation. I can still remember holding their tiny hands for the first time, marveling at their vulnerability and strength. Looking into their faces, I felt an undeniable clarity. If I continued on the path I was on, what kind of example would I be setting for them? They deserved to see a mother who stood tall in her strengths, who led not just with competence but with courage.

It was in that moment that I made a promise to myself and to them. I resolved to stop shrinking. My introversion, I realized, was not the problem; my reluctance to embrace it fully was. I began to see that being an introvert didn't mean I had to stay in the shadows or that it was a weakness. It meant I had to redefine the light I would stand in, one that was authentic to who I was. My natural tendencies, when embraced, weren't constraints but powerful strengths waiting to be unleashed.

The Intersectionality of Being a Black Woman in Corporate America

To give you a full story in its entirety, I must acknowledge an undeniable truth: my lived experience as a Black woman in corporate America adds another layer of complexity to the challenges I have faced. Yes, being an introvert is a significant part of my story, but it intersects with the realities of race and gender in ways that cannot be ignored. My path has been shaped by navigating the complexities of imposter syndrome, microaggressions, shrinking, and code-switching, a constant balancing act to fit into spaces that were not designed with me in mind.

Imposter syndrome is an ever-present whisper, questioning whether I truly belonged at the table, even when my qualifications were undeniable. According to a McKinsey report, 58% of women of color report feeling the need to prove themselves repeatedly in the workplace, compared to 35% of white men. For me, this is often translated into over-preparation, relentless self-critique, and an unwillingness to celebrate my accomplishments.

Microaggressions, those subtle and often unintentional slights, were a recurring backdrop in my career. Comments like, "You're so articulate," meant as a compliment, carried the weight of low expectations. Instances of being overlooked in meetings or having my ideas attributed to others compounded the feeling of invisibility. Research from McKinsey's *Women in the Workplace* report highlights that Black women are more likely than any other group to face these experiences yet are less likely to have allies who advocate for them.

Then there was the shrinking, the quiet, deliberate act of making myself smaller to avoid standing out, and the code-switching, altering my speech, behavior, or appearance to fit the corporate mold. These adaptations were not just survival mechanisms; they were exhausting rituals that slowly eroded my sense of authenticity. The intersection of introversion with these layers of identity made my journey uniquely challenging, yet it also sharpened my resolve to redefine leadership on my terms.

How I Redefined Leadership: Embracing My Quiet Power

Redefining leadership meant embracing my introversion while challenging the narrative that leaders must always be loud, assertive, and extroverted. I focused on leveraging my strengths: strategic thinking, deep listening, emotional intelligence, and thoughtful communication. I also began curating my career with intentionality, selecting roles and projects that aligned with my values and strengths.

I adopted a new mantra: "Lead authentically, influence boldly, and grow strategically." This shift not only transformed my leadership style but also empowered me to inspire others to embrace their unique attributes. By leaning into the S.P.I.C.E. framework, I developed a roadmap for introverts to thrive in leadership roles.

What Is An Introvert: Setting The Record Straight

First, let's set the record straight. An introvert is a person who tends to focus more on their inner thoughts and feelings than seeking external stimulation from social interactions and low-stimulus environments, unlike extroverts who gain energy from being around people. Most people fall somewhere between the extremes of introversion and extroversion, often referred to as ambiverts. Cultural norms and values can influence how introversion is expressed and perceived. For example, individualistic cultures like the U.S. often emphasize extroverted traits, while some collectivist cultures may value quieter, more reflective behaviors associated with introversion. People may misidentify themselves due to societal pressures or misconceptions about what introversion means. For example, some people may consider themselves introverted because they dislike public speaking, but this alone does not define introversion.

Here are some key characteristics of introverts:

1. **Preference for Deep Connections**: They tend to value meaningful, one-on-one conversations over large group interactions or small talk.
2. **Thoughtfulness**: Introverts often think before speaking and are considered reflective and introspective.
3. **Selective Socializing**: They may enjoy social interactions but typically prefer smaller, more intimate gatherings over large crowds.
4. **Inner Focus**: Introverts tend to be more focused on their own thoughts, feelings, and ideas rather than external stimuli.
5. **Sensitivity to Stimulation**: They may find too much noise, activity, or social interaction overwhelming and need downtime to recover.

The biggest misconception is that introversion is a personality trait. It's important to note that being an introvert is not the same as being shy or socially anxious. I am naturally an introvert, I can be an ambivert in social situations, but I am not shy. I have a bold and commanding presence, but I have to be very intentional with my social interactions to preserve energy over time. While shyness relates to fear or discomfort in social situations, introversion is more about how someone processes and gains energy. Now, let's talk about how introverts can lead and advance in their careers. And do it well.

How Introverts Can Excel with S.P.I.C.E.

What is S.P.I.C.E.? A set of principles, a framework to guide leaders on an authentic and strategic journey to effective leadership and career expansion.

- **Savvy**: Combine your talents and expertise with business acumen to leverage a strategic mindset to think big picture and deliver results that matter.
- **Performance**: Delivering excellence intentionally, selecting roles that align with your strengths and values to reduce burnout.
- **Image**: Building an authentic personal brand that inspires trust, has a commanding presence and has credibility.
- **Communication**: Engaging in thoughtful dialogue, clearly articulating the value you deliver, and confidently advocating for yourself.

- **Exposure**: Amplifying your impact through meaningful connections and strategic visibility.

These principles aren't just a framework; they're a call to action. They remind us that leadership is not about conforming to outdated ideals. It's about challenging them. It's about showing that quiet, intentional leadership is just as powerful, if not more than the louder, more traditional models.

1. Savvy: The Strategic Thinker's Edge

Introverts are natural strategists. Our reflective nature enables us to analyze complex problems, anticipate challenges, and devise innovative solutions. Emotional intelligence (EQ), another hallmark of introversion, allows us to build trust and understand team dynamics deeply.

- **The Quiet Strategist:** Introverts excel at stepping back and seeing the big picture. This ability to assess situations holistically is a unique strength in leadership. But being savvy is not just about strategy; it's about understanding the bigger picture to create leverage. Knowing how you make and save your organization money and connecting that to your unique contributions is a game-changer. Leverage gives you confidence and power that doesn't need to be loud or boisterous. The quiet assurance comes from knowing your value and strategically positioning yourself.
- **Leverage Your Strength:** Use your ability to think deeply and observe carefully to identify

opportunities and risks. Position yourself as a thoughtful strategist who connects functional expertise with broader organizational goals. Build confidence by understanding the financial and operational impact of your work.
- **Practical Tip:** Schedule time for strategic reflection. Use tools like SWOT analyses to guide decision-making. Research how your role contributes to your company's bottom line and clearly communicate these insights to your team and stakeholders to amplify your influence.

2. Performance: Excellence Through Focus

Introverts excel at delivering high-quality results through focus and diligence. However, performance is not just about doing the work, it's about doing the right work. To excel without burning out, it's essential to align your efforts with roles and projects that enhance your natural strengths and long-term goals. This is about being intentional: selecting opportunities that highlight your unique abilities while also contributing to your career aspirations.

When you know how you add value, you can make smarter choices about where to direct your energy. This alignment creates a sense of purpose, sustains your performance, and helps you stand out in meaningful ways. Instead of raising your hand for every new project, consider whether the work will showcase your superpowers or simply add to your workload. By focusing on intentional performance, you ensure that your efforts not only deliver results but also elevate your career without compromising your well-being.

- **Intentional Performance:** Introverts thrive when their work aligns with their values and goals. This intentionality creates a sense of purpose and sustains high performance.
- **Leverage Your Strength:** Choose roles and projects that amplify your natural abilities. Avoid overcommitting to tasks that deplete your energy without advancing your career.
- **Practical Tip:** Before taking on new responsibilities, evaluate whether they align with your strengths and career aspirations. Your goal is not to prove whether or not you can multi-task, but to prove you are a strategic asset that adds quantifiable value. Say yes to the "right extras".

3. Image: Crafting an Authentic Leadership Presence

Authenticity is a cornerstone of effective leadership. For introverts, this can mean leaning into your natural charisma, the quiet kind that draws people in because it's genuine and unforced. Crafting an image as a leader isn't about being the loudest in the room; it's about being consistent, relatable, and credible. Introverts excel in these areas because they observe, reflect, and act with purpose. I had to learn how to resist the urge to overtalk the extroverts in meetings. Instead, I leaned into active listening and had private conversations where I could express my ideas and solutions on my terms.

- **The Authentic Leader:** Building an image starts with knowing who you are and what you stand for. Introverts often have a heightened awareness of their values, and when you lead from those values, you create a personal brand that inspires trust and loyalty. Think of your image not as a performance but as an extension of your integrity and authenticity.
- **Leverage Your Strength:** Use your observational skills to tailor your leadership presence. Pay attention to how others perceive you and refine your communication and actions to align with your values. Authenticity builds trust and credibility, and when your words and actions align, people take notice.
- **Practical Tip:** Define three core values that guide your leadership style. Make sure your personal brand, whether through LinkedIn profiles, public speaking, or professional interactions, reflects these values. Pay attention to your presence in meetings or team settings and ask for feedback to ensure you are projecting the authenticity you intend.

4. Communication: The Art of Thoughtful Dialogue and Self-Advocacy

Introverts are masters of thoughtful dialogue. We listen intently, process information deeply, and communicate with intention. However, effective communication for introverted leaders also requires embracing self-advocacy, ensuring that our ideas and contributions are heard and valued. For women, and especially women of color, self-advocacy often comes with unique challenges rooted in societal expectations and systemic biases.

The Thoughtful Communicator: I used to sit in meetings where extroverted colleagues dominated the conversation, speaking quickly and often. Early in my career, I believed I had to match their energy to be seen and heard. I tried to out-talk them, but I soon realized that approach didn't serve me. It drained my energy and diluted my impact.

Instead, I leaned into active listening. While others debated and argued to be the loudest in the room, I would sit quietly, listening for flaws in their arguments and gaps in their ideas. When I finally spoke, it was intentional, precise, and impactful to solve the problem at hand. My colleagues started to notice. The joke became, *"Uh-oh, Shayla's about to speak. She's solved world peace."* It was a lighthearted remark, but it reflected the respect my carefully considered words had earned.

This ability to communicate thoughtfully is a hallmark of introverted leadership. Our words carry weight because they are deliberate and solution focused.

Self-Advocacy as a Woman: For women, advocating for ourselves can sometimes feel like walking a tightrope. Studies show that women who assert themselves may face backlash, often being perceived as overly aggressive or unlikable. As introverts, we can navigate this challenge by leveraging our strengths: being intentional, authentic, and grounded in our values. Self-advocacy doesn't mean compromising who you are; it means confidently articulating your worth and contributions.

As women, we are often told to be humble, grateful, and accommodating. As a Black woman, I was taught not to ruffle feathers, to be seen and not heard, and to be thankful just to have a seat at the table. These messages conditioned me to downplay my contributions and let others take credit for my work.

I vividly remember seeing my ideas adopted and praised, but under someone else's name. I stayed silent because I thought that was the price of professionalism. Over time, this silence cost me more than recognition, it cost me ownership of my career.

For women of color, the stakes are even higher. We are expected to work twice as hard to prove our worth, only to face biases that dismiss or undervalue our efforts. Advocating for ourselves can feel like a rebellion against these ingrained narratives. But it's not just an act of courage; it's an act of reclaiming our power and our narrative. It's about claiming space in environments that may not always welcome our voices and doing so in a way that uplifts others like us.

Leverage Your Strength: Self-advocacy doesn't have to feel boastful. As introverts, we can use our natural skills of observation and preparation to position ourselves effectively. Focus on facts and outcomes when advocating for yourself. Build a "value statement" that connects your contributions to measurable results. For example: *"I* *streamlined this process, saving the team 20 hours per week and increasing productivity by 15%."*

This approach keeps the focus on the value you bring, rather than on personal accolades, which can feel uncomfortable for many introverts.

Practical Strategies & Tips:

- Speak with purpose: In meetings, listen actively and identify the most critical points to address. When you speak, your words will stand out for their clarity and impact. I call this technique "find the flaw." Instead of trying to overtalk the extroverts, find the flaw in their arguments, and you will provide a well-crafted solution that moves the conversation forward.
- Approach communication with a balance of listening and speaking. Use active listening to connect with others, and then thoughtfully advocate for your ideas.
- If you're in a meeting and feel overshadowed, follow up afterward with a recap email or a private conversation to share your insights.

Self-advocacy for women, and particularly for women of color, is not just about being heard. It's about dismantling barriers, challenging biases, and claiming your rightful place as a leader. By blending thoughtful dialogue with purposeful advocacy, you can communicate with authenticity, confidence, and resilience, becoming a leader who inspires and influences through words.

5. Exposure: Strategically Amplify Your Impact

Exposure is often the most challenging element of leadership for women, especially for introverts. Leadership can be isolating, and many women find themselves as the only woman in the room, a reality that can amplify feelings of doubt and alienation. Exposure, however, isn't about being everywhere or knowing everyone; it's about cultivating meaningful relationships and creating opportunities that align with your strengths and goals.

The Strategic Networker: Early in my career, I avoided exposure because I believed my work would speak for itself. I thought that by focusing on delivering results, recognition would naturally follow. Remember those mantras, keep your personal life separate from work, don't make friends and my work lost its identity multiple times. You mean to tell me I have to be visible? I have to attend the happy hours and make friends? But, I learned the hard way that without visibility, even excellent work can go unnoticed. I had to reframe my understanding of exposure, it wasn't about being flashy or self-promotional, but about ensuring my impact was recognized by the right people.

Leadership also taught me how lonely the journey could be. Moving into leadership roles often meant leaving behind familiar peer groups and stepping into spaces where I felt disconnected. I realized that cultivating exposure wasn't just about advancing my career; it was about finding and creating connections that would sustain and support me as a leader.

Building the Right Relationships: To thrive as a leader, you need more than visibility, you need relationships that empower and uplift you. These include:

- **Mentors** who provide guidance and share their experiences.
- **Sponsors** who advocate for you across functions and open doors to new opportunities.
- **Coaches** who challenge you to grow and refine your skills.
- **Accountability partners** who keep you focused and aligned with your goals.
- **Your tribe**, the trusted peers who offer encouragement, perspective, and camaraderie.

These relationships are the foundation of strategic exposure. They ensure you're not navigating leadership in isolation and help amplify your voice in meaningful ways.

Leverage Your Strength: As introverts, we thrive in smaller, more intentional settings. Use your natural ability to build deep, authentic connections to foster relationships that matter. Focus on quality over quantity and create opportunities for mutual growth and collaboration.

Practical Tips for Exposure:

- **Start with intentional connections**: Identify mentors and sponsors who align with your goals. Build relationships over time by showing genuine interest in their expertise and sharing your vision.
- **Expand your visibility strategically**: Volunteer for cross-functional projects or initiatives that showcase

your skills and allow you to work with leaders outside your immediate circle.
- **Nurture your tribe**: Develop a support network of peers who understand your journey and can provide encouragement and accountability. Regularly connect with them to share wins, challenges, and advice.
- **Share your value**: Use platforms like LinkedIn, team meetings, or presentations to highlight your contributions. This isn't about boasting; it's about ensuring your impact is visible and recognized.

The Amplifying Power of Connection: One of the most transformative lessons I've learned is that leadership is not a solo journey. Your network of mentors, sponsors, coaches, accountability partners, and peers plays a critical role in amplifying your voice, providing perspective, and creating opportunities you might not have found on your own.

Exposure isn't about being in every room, it's about being in the right rooms, with the right people, and ensuring your work and leadership are seen and valued. By building strategic relationships and redefining exposure on your terms, you can amplify your impact while staying authentic to yourself.

Conclusion

Leadership as we know it needs to evolve. For too long, we've upheld a narrow definition of what leadership looks like: loud, extroverted, and often performative. But the realities of today's workplaces and the complexities of a global, diverse workforce demand something more. The reality is that leadership comes in many forms, and the quiet power of introverts is just as vital and impactful.

It's time to redefine leadership.

Redefining leadership means moving beyond outdated ideals and embracing a broader, more inclusive standard. It's about recognizing that leadership isn't just about being seen or heard, it's about creating meaningful impact. It's about balancing authenticity with influence, thoughtfulness with decisiveness, and boldness with humility.

For introverts, leadership begins by embracing who we are, strategic thinkers, deep listeners, and reflective decision-makers. The S.P.I.C.E. framework isn't about becoming someone we're not; it's about leaning into the unique qualities that make us exceptional leaders. It's about redefining success, authenticity, and impact in ways that honor our natural strengths.

But let's be honest: the road isn't always easy. The corporate world often rewards the loudest voices and the boldest personas. As women, especially as women who find themselves as the only ones in the room, the journey can feel isolating. We are faced with unspoken pressures to conform, to shrink, or to overcompensate. The challenge is not just to survive in these spaces but to thrive authentically.

Thriving authentically means shifting our focus from fitting into existing molds to creating spaces where our strengths are celebrated. It means advocating for ourselves unapologetically, building relationships that amplify our impact, and setting boundaries that protect our energy. It's about standing firm in our values and leading with integrity.

My journey has taught me that being an introvert isn't a limitation; it's a superpower. Deep thinking, emotional intelligence, and the ability to listen and connect on a profound level are not just traits; they are leadership essentials. When we embrace them fully, we can create workplaces that value substance over style, thoughtfulness over noise, and authenticity over conformity.

To all the introverted leaders reading this: your voice matters. Your perspective matters. Your leadership matters. The world needs leaders who think deeply, act thoughtfully, and inspire others through authenticity and purpose.

This is your invitation to step into your power. Lead with your strengths. Lead with authenticity. Lead with S.P.I.C.E.

And remember, you don't have to shout to make an impact. Sometimes, the quietest voices create the most profound change.

The journey to redefine leadership is not one I've taken alone. This anthology brings together the voices of extraordinary leaders who, in their own ways, have challenged conventional norms and rewritten the rules of what it means to lead. Each author brings a unique perspective, shaped by their lived experiences, professional triumphs, and lessons learned in the trenches.

So, turn the page, meet the next author, and prepare to step into a reimagined world of leadership.

About the Author

Shayla N. Atkins

Award-winning Leadership Expert | Workplace Culture Strategist | CEO of The Atkins IMPACT Consulting Firm | Best-Selling Author

As the accomplished best-selling author of *Black Women Lead With S.P.I.C.E.*, Shayla N. Atkins expands the S.P.I.C.E. leadership development ecosystem and inspires leaders to embrace authenticity as the ultimate leadership currency. She shares actionable insights through her LinkedIn newsletter, *The Culture Compass,* and her strategies have been featured in over 100 publications and major media outlets, including *The CW, Forbes, USA Today,* and more.

A sought-after speaker, Shayla has taken the stage at the nation's largest events, including the SHRM Annual Conference, Women in Trucking Accelerate Expo, Women's Energy Network, and Essence Festival, just to name a few. Her authentic delivery, poignant storytelling, and practical tools have made her a trusted voice in leadership, moving audiences across the country from theory and motivation to action.

Shayla is a former Fortune 500 executive, a global leader in leadership development, workplace culture transformation, and organizational effectiveness. With over two decades of private sector experience and a proven track record of driving measurable outcomes, Shayla has redefined how organizations achieve growth, innovation, and transformation.

As the CEO and Founder of The Atkins IMPACT Consulting Firm, Shayla leads a dynamic team dedicated to equipping operational industries, including oil and gas, manufacturing, construction, and tech—with the tools and strategies to cultivate inclusive and effective cultures, retain top talent, and build high-performing teams.

In 2022, Shayla was honored with the *Presidential Lifetime Achievement Award* by President Joseph R. Biden, recognizing her extraordinary contributions of over 4,000 hours of community service. Her work reflects her mission to level the playing field for authentic people to thrive and deliver results.

Shayla's career began in senior leadership roles at Fortune 500 companies, where she honed her expertise in strategic HR leadership, diversity and inclusion, and cultural transformation. A Lean Six Sigma Black Belt and Prosci Certified Change Leader, she combines data-driven solutions with a human-centered approach to address complex organizational challenges. Her firm specializes in leadership development, workplace culture effectiveness strategies, cultural assessments, and professional development for women leaders. Focused on mid-size to large organizations, The Atkins IMPACT Consulting Firm delivers tailored strategies that produce lasting business results.

Shayla N. Atkins is not just a leader; she is a catalyst for change, redefining leadership and setting new standards for excellence in the modern workplace.

Contact Information:

Shayla N. Atkins
Email: Info@theatkinsimpact.com
Company website: www.theatkinsimpact.com
LinkedIn: www.linkedin.com/in/shayla-n-atkins

THE POWER OF STRATEGIC LEADERSHIP

Savvy leadership is the key to elevating your career and leading with impact. It's what separates those who simply do the work from those who drive the vision. Advancing in leadership requires more than expertise; it demands business acumen, the ability to see the big picture, anticipate challenges, and position yourself strategically for opportunities. Business savvy enhances your talents and experience, giving you the leverage to move from executing tasks to shaping strategy, from being a high-performing contributor to leading high-performing teams.

Leadership today requires more than just keeping up; it demands the foresight to stay ahead, to innovate, and to inspire others to do the same.

In the chapters ahead, our authors will guide you through the mindset shifts, decision-making frameworks, and strategic positioning that will help you step into senior leadership with confidence, influence at a higher level, and make the transition from tactical expert to visionary leader.

Chapter 2

Breaking the Mold in a Male-Dominated World

Lessons in Redefining Leadership

Melissa Mack

How do you rise and succeed in an industry that was not designed with you in mind?

When I look back on my career in security, a male-dominated field that often feels unyielding, I realize my journey has been anything but traditional. I didn't start as a police officer or serve in the military like most of my colleagues. When I tell people I've worked in security management for 25 years, their reactions are often the same: surprise, curiosity, and sometimes disbelief. "Oh, that's…different. How'd YOU get into that?" they say. They're right, it is not a common profession, and this industry wasn't built for women. It's male-dominated, law enforcement or military-influenced, and steeped in traditions that don't often make space for people like me. *I began as a wide-eyed young woman with a love for crime shows and an even bigger love for justice.* My story isn't about fitting into the mold of the security industry, it's about breaking it and forging my own path.

The journey wasn't easy, and it didn't follow a straight path. I had to fight for my place, learn to trust my voice, and embrace what made me different. But the struggles also shaped me, showing me how to lead authentically and helping me redefine what leadership looks like in this space. My story isn't just about my career, it's about resilience, perspective, and the lessons I've learned along the way.

The Spark That Lit the Flame

I didn't grow up dreaming of working in security. My fascination with criminal justice began with TV shows like Murder, She Wrote, In the Heat of the Night, and Columbo. I'd sit cross-legged on the living room floor, captivated by the idea of uncovering the truth and solving puzzles. But it wasn't just TV that shaped my perspective; it was also my family. My mom, a white woman raised in the backwoods of Louisiana, grew up in a world where rivers literally divided Black and White communities. She often told stories of the systemic racism she witnessed against people, and those stories planted seeds of awareness in me. But this awareness and passion became personal during a high school experience I'll never forget.

One night, two friends, who were Black, picked me up in one of their old-school Camaros. We were heading to a house party, music blasting from the speakers. It was one of those nights where the world feels alive, and you're young enough to think nothing bad can happen, especially in a familiar neighborhood we had perused through countless numbers of times. Then, the flashing lights appeared in the rearview mirror.

At first, I didn't think much of it. My mom had been pulled over plenty of times for speeding (she has a heavy foot), so I assumed this would be the same, a routine stop. But it wasn't. The officer ordered my friend who was driving out of the car, and before I knew it, backup arrived. They searched the car, questioned us, and treated us with aggression that left me shaken. My friend hadn't been speeding. He hadn't done anything wrong. After 45 minutes, we were free to go with a "warning". To this day, I still don't know what for.

That night was my first real glimpse into systemic bias. I saw how different the world could be for people who didn't look like me. It opened my eyes to the injustice my mom had spoken about and left me with a burning question: How could I be a force for change?

The Road Less Traveled

By the time I went to college, I was determined to make a difference. I majored in criminal justice, envisioning a future in law enforcement. My plan was clear: graduate, join the Police Department, and advocate for fairness and justice from the inside. But life rarely goes according to plan.

During my senior year, an Asset Protection Lead from Target visited my college to talk about their asset protection program. He described a role that combined my interest in criminal justice with business, a space I hadn't even considered. The idea intrigued me. It wasn't law enforcement, but it was still about protecting people and uncovering the truth. So, I took a leap and joined Target after graduation.

At first, my days were spent catching shoplifters, investigating employee theft, and setting up covert cameras. It wasn't glamorous, but it was an on-the-job learning experience. I learned about risk, security tactics, and what it meant to protect an organization's assets. Over the years, I worked my way up, moving from one retail organization to another, building asset protection programs, and learning every corner of the industry.

But by 2010, I could see the writing on the wall, and I started to see the industry changing. The rise of e-commerce and Amazon meant brick-and-mortar stores were facing new challenges. I realized that if I wanted to stay relevant and marketable, I'd need to pivot, learn new skills, and prepare for a future that looked very different from the one I'd started in. Over the years my business acumen strengthened, and I'd learn to pay attention to industry and market trends. This knowledge gave me the control I needed to chart my own path and change course on my terms. That decision set the stage for the next chapter of my career.

When Purpose Meets Opportunity

One of the most pivotal moments in my journey came during one of the most challenging times in my life. I had just gone through a divorce, leaving me as a single mom to my one-year-old son. I'd recently earned my master's degree in leadership and management, but even with a full-time job, I couldn't make ends meet.

My days were a blur of work, daycare drop-offs, and repeat. I couldn't afford both my mortgage and my son's daycare, so I started teaching night classes in criminal justice and security management at a local college to bring in extra income. It was exhausting, teaching after a long day of work, lesson planning late into the night. Teaching wasn't something I'd planned on, but it turned out to be one of the most transformative experiences of my career. Standing in front of a classroom forced me to grow. I had to learn public speaking, how to engage an audience, articulate complex ideas, and think on my feet. It gave me confidence I didn't know I needed.

One night, while preparing a lesson, I found a reference to a global security management professional organization in a textbook. I'd never heard of it before, so I did some research. It was the premier organization for security professionals, with a local chapter near me. Curious, I attended one of their events.

Walking into that room, I felt out of place. Most of the attendees were men, many with significant, tenured backgrounds, including federal law enforcement. But as I listened to their conversations and stories, I realized something: I had something to offer, too. My retail security background, leadership experience, and ability to think strategically were just as valuable as their tactical expertise. I began to see the broader possibilities within the security industry.

The following year, I scraped together the money and attended the association's global conference. I paid my own way, took vacation days, and stepped into a world I didn't fully understand yet, and it was a game-changer. Fifteen thousand professionals from around the world came together to discuss cutting-edge technology, risk management, and the future of security. I soaked up every moment, attending sessions, networking, and learning as much as I could. That conference opened my eyes to the full potential of my career, the exposure changed the trajectory of my journey and my life. Today, I sit on the certification board for that same association, helping shape the future of the industry I once felt on the outskirts of.

Thriving in Male-Dominated Spaces

Being a woman in security is like walking into a room where the playbook was written for someone else. Early in my career, I'd attend networking events where I'd be one of only three women in a crowd of 75 men. Many of my male colleagues, with backgrounds in law enforcement or the military, often approached leadership through a command-driven, tactical lens. What I didn't fully realize at the time was how deeply ingrained the barriers were, not just in the day-to-day dynamics but in the systems that shaped the entire industry.

It was designed around traits often associated with traditional male leadership and delivery styles: authority, tactical problem solving, hierarchical thinking, and a command and-control mindset. Early on, I felt the pressure to emulate these traits. I thought if I didn't conform, I wouldn't succeed, so that's exactly what I did. Early on, I struggled with imposter syndrome, thinking I didn't have their backgrounds, and I worried I wouldn't measure up. The few women I saw in the industry often felt the need to adopt a "hard edge" to survive, myself included. We were tough, gritty, and determined to prove we could keep up with the men. But trying to follow that playbook only left me feeling out of place, exhausted, and stuck.

I've experienced moments where my ideas were overlooked until a male colleague echoed them. I've sat in meetings where my expertise was questioned, not because of my qualifications but because of my gender. One of the most subtle but pervasive challenges is the assumption that women must constantly prove their competence. While my male counterparts could rely on their titles or backgrounds to command respect, I had to earn it over and over again. But instead of letting this discourage me, I've learned to use it as fuel.

It took time and a lot of self-reflection to realize that my value didn't lie in trying to be like everyone else but in being myself. I realized my differences were my strengths. I brought something to the table that was sorely needed: emotional intelligence, empathy, the ability to build relationships, and a collaborative approach to problem-solving. What I thought I was missing was exactly what I needed to excel; I just had to lean into it. I've learned to advocate for myself, articulate the value I deliver, and hold my ground when necessary. I've also leaned into mentorship and using my experiences to help other women navigate these challenges.

The security industry still has a long way to go in achieving gender equity, but change is happening, one conversation, one ally, and one demonstration of excellence at a time. For me, thriving in this space has been about more than just my own individual success. It's about creating opportunities for the next generation of women to step into these roles with confidence. To any woman considering a career in security, I say this: Your voice matters. Your perspective matters. And while the road may be tough, it's worth walking. Leadership in this industry isn't about fitting into the mold, it's about reshaping it.

Lessons from My Journey: Turning Insights into Action

Although my journey has been challenging, it has imparted valuable insights into leadership and authenticity. The lessons weren't handed to me, they were earned in moments of doubt, triumph, and determination. Here's how I learned to navigate a male-dominated world and find success on my terms, paired with practical strategies, tips and stories that bring these lessons to life.

1. **Know Who You Are; and Own It**

In the early years of my career, I often felt like an outsider. Their paths looked nothing like mine, and for a while, I thought that meant I didn't belong. I remember sitting at a networking event, surrounded by men swapping global war stories about tactical missions and high-pressure situations. Meanwhile, my "story" was about teenagers stealing cell phones. I felt small, out of place, and frankly, invisible. But then I started asking myself some hard questions: Why was I letting their paths define my worth? What did I bring to the table that they didn't? After all, I had significantly contributed to the store's profitability by reducing shrinkage and fostering a safe environment for both employees and customers. Slowly, I began to realize that my unique experiences were a strength, not a weakness. They were my competitive advantage, not my pitfalls. For example, my retail background taught me how to understand human behavior in real time, build systems from the ground up, and manage complex teams. While others leaned on tactical experience, I leaned on emotional intelligence and leadership, skills that were often missing from the conversations around me.

Tactical Tips:
- **Perform a Personal SWOT Analysis:** Identify your strengths, weaknesses, opportunities, and threats. Reflect on your unique value and how it can align with your workplace challenges. For me, understanding my emotional intelligence as a strength allowed me to lead with empathy rather than authority.
- **Define Your Leadership Style:** Don't try to replicate someone else's approach. Instead, lean into the traits that resonate with you. My approach became a balance of strategic thinking and emotional

connection, qualities that set me apart in the security industry.
- **Create a Leadership Statement:** Articulate what you stand for as a leader. My statement became clear: " I lead with integrity, solving challenges through collaboration and innovation while building trust with key stakeholders."

2. **Find and Fill the Gaps**

Leadership isn't about doing what's already being done or maintaining the status quo—it's about finding the gaps and filling them in ways only you can. Every workplace has gaps—areas where needs are unmet, perspectives are missing, or opportunities for improvement exist. **The key is identifying those gaps and positioning yourself as the solution**. This strategy has been a game-changer for me, especially in an industry that undervalues essential soft skills like empathy, active listening, adaptability, and conflict resolution to complement the tactical skillsets. It's all in perspective.

Tactical Tips
- **Observe and Ask Questions:** Pay attention to recurring challenges in your organization. Is there a communication breakdown? A lack of inclusivity? An unmet operational need? In one of my earlier roles, I noticed that while my peers focused on tactical security, no one was addressing cross-functional collaboration, a gap I was uniquely equipped to fill.

- **Build Cross-Functional Expertise**: Diversify your skill set so you can address gaps beyond your immediate role. For example, I expanded my knowledge of risk management, business continuity, and financial management which helped me bridge the tactical and strategic aspects of security and business.
- **Present Solutions with Data:** When you identify a gap, back up your recommendations with data, benchmarking, and case studies.

3. Embrace Resilience As Your Superpower

Resilience is often talked about as the ability to "bounce back," but in leadership, it's about more than that, it's the capacity to adapt, grow, and push forward even when the odds are stacked against you. As one of only two female regional security managers for an iconic, global Fortune 500 corporation, I knew I'd face scrutiny. But I didn't anticipate just how often I'd be questioned about my decisions, my qualifications, and even my presence in the room.

There were days I left meetings feeling defeated, wondering if I was cut out for this. But every time I felt like giving up, I reminded myself of why I was there: my unwavering commitment to safeguarding people and assets, paving the way for other women, showing that leadership doesn't have to look one way, and proving to myself that I belonged. For women, especially in industries where we're underrepresented, resilience is not optional. it's essential.

Tactical Tips
- **Develop a Resilience Toolkit:** Build a personal set of practices to help you recover and stay focused. For me, this includes taking my earned PTO, regular exercise, and maintaining a strong support system of mentors and peers.
- **Preparation is Key:** Being proactive and prepared builds resilience, enabling effective and composed responses to unexpected challenges. When I was notified of a medical emergency in my store's women's restroom, I discovered an unresponsive customer. I immediately enacted our emergency response protocols, performed CPR, and maintained a calm and focused demeanor throughout the incident.
- **Practice Reframing:** Learn to view obstacles as opportunities for growth. When I was underestimated due to my retail background, I reframed it as an advantage, emphasizing my diverse experience and problem-solving skills.

Resilience is also about finding your support system. For me, that meant connecting with other women in the industry, mentors, peers, and allies who understood the challenges I was facing. They reminded me that I wasn't alone and that every small victory mattered.

4. Build Your Business Savvy and Acumen: Understand the Bigger Picture

In an industry like security, where tactical skills often take center stage, developing business acumen has been one of my most powerful tools for standing out and increasing my impact. Early on, I realized that understanding the business wasn't just about knowing security protocols, it was about grasping the broader organizational goals, market trends, and the needs of the clients we served.

Business savvy isn't about being the smartest person in the room, it's about understanding the room, anticipating needs, and aligning your efforts with the goals of those around you. It's about seeing beyond your own role and thinking like a leader. For me, developing business acumen has been a journey of curiosity and continuous learning. It's what allowed me to pivot when the industry shifted, build lasting relationships, and rise to a leadership role in a field where women are still the minority.

The lesson here is simple: to lead effectively, you must know more than just your job, you must know the business. When you do, you not only elevate your own career but also create opportunities to make a greater impact. Leadership isn't just about what you do; it's about how you connect, contribute, and create value for the world around you.

Tactical Tips
- **Understand Your Industry and Clients:** Learn how your industry operates, how your company makes, spends, and saves money, and how it connects to your clients' goals. For me, this meant

staying ahead of market trends, like the rise of e-commerce and the shift toward risk mitigation and resilience planning. By understanding these shifts, I was able to anticipate client needs and position myself as a forward-thinking leader.

- **Connect Security to Business Outcomes:** Don't focus solely on security or your specific function's metrics; tie your efforts to broader business objectives like revenue growth, operational efficiency, and risk reduction. For instance, I positioned a workplace violence prevention program as a strategic initiative to enhance employee morale, boost productivity, and safeguard brand reputation, all directly supporting the company's bottom line, which resonated with executive leadership.
- **Leverage Data and Insights:** Use data to tell compelling stories and drive decision-making. Whether it's presenting industry trends, risk assessments, or projections, shows how your work aligns with and supports the organization's strategic goals.

Conclusion

When I reflect on my journey, I see a path paved with challenges, resilience, and a determination to lead authentically. I didn't rise to where I am by conforming to someone else's expectations or playbook. Instead, I learned to embrace who I am, identify opportunities, and position myself as a leader who adds value in ways only I can. These lessons, owning your identity, finding and filling gaps, harnessing resilience, and mastering business acumen, are more than just strategies for success. They are a call to action for anyone navigating spaces that weren't designed for them. Whether you're stepping into a male-dominated industry, pushing against systemic barriers, or simply seeking to grow, remember: Leadership is not about blending in. It's about influence and leading with intention.

Here's my challenge to you:
- **Know Your Value:** Your unique perspective and skills are your superpower. Embrace them. Stand firm in who you are and let that authenticity guide you.
- **Be a Problem Solver:** Look for opportunities to make an impact. Whether it's addressing a gap in your workplace or bringing innovative ideas to the table, don't wait for permission to lead.
- **Build Resilience:** When challenges come, and they will, lean into your strength. Use every setback as an opportunity to grow and prove your value. True growth, both personal and professional, begins outside of your comfort zone.
- **Think Like a Business Leader:** Understanding the broader goals of your organization and industry isn't just a skill; it's a pivotal advantage. When you connect your work to the big picture, you elevate yourself as a trusted advisor.

The future of leadership is being redefined every day by people like you and me, people who dare to be different, who bring authenticity to the table, and who lead with empathy and adaptability. So, what will you do next? Will you take that leap of faith? Will you step into a space that challenges you? Will you choose to lead not just for yourself but for those who will follow in your footsteps? The world needs leaders who redefine what's possible. It needs you. Take the lessons, take the leap, and take your place as the leader you were always meant to be.

About the Author

Melissa Mack

Global Security Strategist | Advocate for Diversity in Leadership | Transformational Risk Management Expert

Melissa Mack is a distinguished force in global security management, with a career spanning over 25 years of transformative leadership in risk mitigation, crisis management, and asset protection. A Certified Protection Professional (CPP), Melissa is renowned for her ability to develop innovative strategies that protect people, organizations, and reputations while fostering inclusive and resilient workplace cultures.

Melissa's career began in retail loss prevention, where her innovative use of analytics delivered substantial reductions in shrinkage, setting a new standard for operational success. Her trajectory includes leadership roles at iconic global organizations. At McDonald's, she spearheaded the development of the U.S. Workplace Violence Prevention Program, addressing critical security needs with precision and compassion. At Willis Towers Watson, she managed global security policies across 120 countries, ensuring organizational alignment and operational excellence. Currently, as Managing Director for Pinkerton Consulting & Investigations, Melissa leads initiatives that elevate enterprise security risk management strategies, enhance operational efficiencies, and deliver measurable client impact.

A lifelong learner and industry advocate, Melissa holds a Master's in Criminal Justice Leadership and Management and a Bachelor's in Criminal Justice from Sam Houston State University. Her passion for advancing the profession is evident in her service on the ASIS Professional Certification Board, where she champions rigorous security standards and certifications. Beyond her professional expertise, Melissa is a certified résumé writer and interview coach, dedicated to empowering professionals to achieve their career aspirations.

Melissa's unwavering commitment to diversity and allyship has positioned her as a leading advocate for women in security. She has earned accolades such as McDonald's U.S. Security Professional of the Year through her innovative leadership and advocacy.

As a co-author of *Leadership Redefined*, Melissa draws from her remarkable career to offer compelling insights on navigating male-dominated industries, driving meaningful change, and building resilient, high-performing teams. Her chapter inspires readers to lead with authenticity, courage, and integrity.

Melissa Mack exemplifies what it means to lead with purpose, influence boldly, and transform challenges into opportunities, setting a global benchmark for excellence in security and leadership.

Contact Information:

Melissa Mack
melmack019@gmail.com
https://www.linkedin.com/in/melissa-mack-cpp-cprw
https://www.facebook.com/share/1Jxo9Y384e/

Chapter 3

The Savvy Culture Leader

Balancing Heart and Head for Transformational Impact

Mildred Black

"People will forget what you said, people will forget what you did, but people will never forget how you made them feel."

Maya Angelou

In the chaotic and uncertain bustle of corporate life, where quarterly reports, deadlines, and performance metrics often dominate the conversation, one powerful truth refuses to be overshadowed: how leaders make their people feel. Imagine an organization where employees wake up excited to do their work, not just because of a paycheck or a line on a resume but because they feel genuinely valued. Consider the ripple effects on families, communities, and customers when leaders step beyond titles and into genuine connection.

Now, ask yourself a simple yet profound question: **What if your success as a leader depends on the quality of your decisions and your ability to shape the unseen culture within your organization?**

This chapter invites you to explore the transformative journey of becoming a savvy culture leader who balances the head (strategy, data, performance) with the heart (empathy, trust, connection). Drawing on personal stories, research findings, and practical frameworks, we will delve into the art and science of leadership that transcends mere profit margins and resonates at the human level.

Introduction

Leading people is an art, science, and spirit. In modern organizations, metrics and financial returns typically grab the spotlight. Still, there is growing recognition that leadership's "soft stuff" empathy, trust, and genuine connection- is not soft at all. Instead, it is the hardest part to master and the most powerful in achieving sustainable success (Buckingham & Goodall, 2022).

This chapter seeks to illuminate that path. We will examine the critical role of empathy in leadership, the necessity of integrating it into an existing culture before attempting to change it, and how a focus on people-first leadership naturally leads to higher performance. We will also explore my journey through adversity, coping with multiple sclerosis (MS), a family health crisis, and an informal 360-degree review that showed me how disconnected my leadership had become leading to a profound shift from results-centric leadership to relationship-centric leadership.

Along the way, we will see how data and accountability remain essential tools. Inspired by Peter Drucker's (1974) classic adage, "What gets measured gets managed," we will learn to measure what matters, but also to remember that measuring is not enough. In the end, the synergy of art (heart, empathy, connection) and science (data, metrics, systems) elevates leaders into the realm of the "savvy culture leader," changing not only workplace outcomes but the lives of everyone involved.

The Foundation of My Career: A Technical Journey

I started my professional journey immersed in the technical world. Having studied electrical engineering before finishing a degree in finance, I was fascinated by data-driven results. I thrived on leading projects, implementing programs and systems, writing code to measure productivity, establishing systems to monitor outcomes, and integrating new technologies to increase efficiency. Early on, I worked in retail (Target Stores) as an HR manager and later moved into technology and healthcare settings, using my technical background to create daily productivity management tools. These tools precisely tracked patient volumes, measured daily output, and analyzed performance metrics. Data was like a compass, steady, objective, and reliable.

Beyond my fascination with numbers, I also had a personal motivation. Growing up in rural Alabama as the child of a single mother, I experienced scarcity firsthand. Those early experiences with hardship sharpened my ambition to build a more secure future, an ambition that crystallized when I saw how my aunt and uncle's comfortable lifestyle, made possible through engineering and business, could offer me a tangible path to success.

Observing my aunt and uncle, Aunt Monica and Uncle Tyrone, an aerospace engineer, living a comfortable lifestyle convinced me that a career in engineering or business would provide a pathway to a prosperous life. My early successes in developing business systems, leading projects, and measuring productivity were satisfying. Yet I soon found that my focus on tasks and results overshadowed the opportunity to tap into and optimize something more vital: connecting with the people who brought those metrics to life.

The Reality Check

In retrospect, I was highly motivated to prove myself, partly shaped by being oftentimes the only woman and/or African American in certain leadership rooms. I expected the highest possible results from my teams. While this intensity often delivered short-term gains, it ultimately created an environment where my team members felt burned out and stressed out. The pivotal moment occurred when I recognized that, despite my technical proficiencies, I was lacking what Stephen Covey (1989) refers to as "synergy," a fortuitous realm where "one plus one equals ten, a hundred, or even a thousand!" (p. 262).

We were performing, yet I missed the heart connection with some of my team members. We hit targets, but I missed out on forging meaningful relationships. Some team members I led felt like mere cogs in a machine rather than collaborators on a shared mission. I was devastated when I realized the impact I was having on my team. The dissonance set the stage for a life-changing wake-up call.

The Diagnosis and the Personal Crisis

Life can force us to pause in the most unexpected ways. For me, that moment arrived with a diagnosis of multiple sclerosis (MS). I had been experiencing dizzy spells, headaches, and eventually the loss of vision in my left eye, which led me to see a neurologist. At one point, I wore an eye patch at work as I was awaiting test results. Over the next five years, I dealt with temporary vision interruptions, struggles with movement, and neurological pain. Adding to the emotional strain, my mother spent 30 days in the ICU battling pancreatitis, and during this time, I suffered a miscarriage.

This combination of personal crises, MS, a severe family health scare, and a miscarriage, brought my world to a halt. When I could barely walk or felt fear for my mother's life, no metric or performance target mattered. The fragility of life became painfully apparent, and I realized how quickly everything can crumble when one's health and family stability are threatened.

In the aftermath of grappling with these health scares, I found myself facing a different kind of upheaval at work, one that would ultimately force me to confront my leadership style head-on.

The Professional Reckoning: A Scathing 360-Degree Review

On the heels of these personal battles came a professional earthquake: an informal 360-degree review from my team revealed that I was a source of disconnect. I was so focused on achieving my goals that I missed the importance of human connection. My staff felt overworked, unseen, and demotivated.

The numbers from that review felt even harsher than my medical diagnosis. Reading statements that I was creating a workaholic culture stung deeply, particularly as I prided myself on delivering results. According to a 2023 research report by DDI, leaders who utilize 360-degree feedback are 8 times more likely to be seen as effective by their teams. However, at that moment, it felt like a personal indictment.

Eye-Opening Statistics About Engagement and Empathy

Beyond my own story, the broader data supports why empathy and connection matter:

1. Gallup's State of the Global Workplace 2024 found that only 23% of employees globally are engaged at work, yet engaged employees are 18% more productive (Gallup, 2023).

2. Businessolver's (2024) State of Workplace Empathy Report found that 88% of employees are more likely to stay with an empathetic employer. In addition, 52% of employees say they'd be willing to take slightly less pay to work for a more empathetic employer, a five-point increase from the previous year. In addition, 67% of employees are willing to work longer hours for an empathetic employer.

The data underscores that an empathetic, people-centered approach is a proven solution we can all access.

Turning Point: A Convergence of Diagnosis and Self-Discovery

My multiple sclerosis diagnosis served as a clear wake-up call that I was making choices that were detrimental to my well-being, my body was reacting to the unhealthy path I had chosen. Simultaneously, the workaholic in me was propelled by fear, seeking to avoid any hint of imperfection. The health crises, compounded with a challenging 360-degree review, ultimately served as a wake-up call, calling me back to my authentic self. It was a wake-up call to love myself enough to show up more fully as me for my team and the work I genuinely care about. I wish I could say it was an epiphany or an instantaneous transformation, but it wasn't. It took me years to grasp what truly happened and why. Over time, I came to realize that real and authentic leadership calls for self-awareness, self-compassion, and a willingness to align my values with my actions.

Lessons Learned: Insights from My Journey

I discovered the power of carving out time for authentic, one-on-one conversations with my team rather than disappearing into endless deliverables and to-do lists. Asking open-ended questions like "How are you, really?" or "What can I do to support your goals?" helped me cultivate deeper relationships and truly understand the people I was leading. I also realized how crucial it is to confront fear, particularly the fear of failure that was intensified by being the "only one" in my demographic. Authentic leadership, I've learned, involves embracing vulnerability and trusting your team to rise to the challenge alongside you.

After navigating through these personal challenges, I gained a renewed understanding of the crucial aspects of leadership.

Here are the strategies, tips, and advice I've gathered, backed by my experiences and further research:

Leading With Heart and Mind

1. **Recognize Culture as an Existing Force**

    - **Observation Before Influence**
      Leadership exists within a cultural context that predates your arrival (Buckingham & Goodall, 2022). Whether you're new to a department or an

entire organization, observe its norms, values, and unspoken rules. A savvy culture leader integrates first and influences second.

- **Power of Assimilation**
  Understanding the existing culture helps you identify where to bring positive change without causing alienation. Embrace humility. Ask questions like, "What traditions here are most important to protect?" and "What do employees value most about this culture?"

2. Prioritize Empathy as an Essential Skill

- **Empathy as a Superpower**
  Empathy is not a weakness; it is the strongest connector. Taking the time to see your team as individuals with unique stories creates a psychological safety net where people feel empowered to voice concerns, share ideas, and innovate.
- **Active Listening Techniques**
  Practice repeating what you hear or asking clarifying questions. Body language (eye contact, leaning in slightly, nodding) signals genuine interest, which quickly fosters trust.
- **Statistics for Conviction**
  In a 2022 *State of Workplace Empathy* report, **93%** of employees said they're more likely to stay with an empathetic employer (Businessolver, 2022). This is not just a "nice idea", it's an **organizational advantage**.

3. Manage What Matters: Data and Metrics

- **Define Clear Goals**
  Inspired by Peter Drucker (1974), start with clarity. Ask yourself, "What outcomes are we driving toward?" Break these down into department-specific, measurable goals that each team member can understand and take ownership of.
- **Set Critical Success Factors**
  Outline the conditions and resources needed to achieve goals. This might include adequate staff training, budget allocations, or cross-departmental collaboration. According to a 2022 Gallup study, clarity around roles and expectations is often a top driver of engagement (Gallup, 2023).
- **Establish a Cadence of Accountability**
  Review progress regularly through structured meetings or reports. This consistency ensures you stay on track and allows timely course corrections rather than last-minute scrambles.

4. Embrace Feedback

- **Participate in 360-Degree Reviews**
  As painful as it was, the informal 360 feedback I received transformed my leadership style. According to *The Society of Human Resources Management* (2024), organizations using 360-degree feedback experienced an average performance improvement of 14.9%. Consistent feedback loops encourage transparency and promote continuous learning and growth.

- **Personal Reflection**
  Develop a habit of journaling or private reflection to process both positive and negative feedback. Ask yourself, "What pattern am I seeing here, and how does it align with my personal values?"

5. Leverage Varied Perspectives

- **Celebrate Different Viewpoints**
  According to McKinsey & Company's (2023) *Women in the Workplace* study, companies with more than 30% female executives tend to outperform those with fewer female leaders. This highlights the tangible benefits of diverse perspectives. When you bring together people from different backgrounds, you enrich decision-making and strengthen the entire organization's collective intelligence.

- **Recognize You Belong**
  If you ever find yourself as the only person of your demographic in a leadership room, remember that you're meant to be there. Your unique viewpoint is a valuable resource, sparking resilience, empathy, and creativity. By fully participating and sharing your experiences, you help shape an environment where every voice is heard and every contribution is acknowledged. In this way, you're fostering a culture of respect and openness that benefits the team and the organization as a whole.

Where I Am Now

Today, I serve as a workplace transformation architect, leveraging my role as the creator of The Culture Model™ and the HEART Model™ to guide senior leaders toward both sustainable performance outcomes and personal and professional fulfillment. After years of navigating the complexities of team dynamics, organizational culture, and personal challenges, I've learned that the most meaningful progress occurs when we balance empathy with accountability. My work now centers on equipping leaders to develop people-first strategies, foster vibrant workplace cultures, and achieve results that endure, both for the organization and the individuals who power its success. I remain committed to continuous learning, both professionally by staying updated on performance management and organizational psychology trends and personally by reflecting on how I can lead with heart and head.

Conclusion & Reflection

The journey from a purely task-focused, data-driven manager to a savvy culture leader is neither simple nor instantaneous. It often requires a wake-up call, like a serious illness, a scathing 360-degree review, or a plateau in organizational performance, to illuminate our blind spots. Yet every challenge can become a crucible for transformation.

Here are some questions to spark your own reflection:

1. **Task vs. Relationship**
   Which do you naturally prioritize? How might you rebalance your attention to embrace performance metrics and authentic connections?
2. **Cultural Integration**
   What unspoken norms exist in your organization, and how can you integrate with them before trying to initiate change?
3. **Empathy in Practice**
   How comfortable are you with showing vulnerability in leadership? What specific steps can you take to demonstrate genuine empathy?
4. **Performance Metrics**
   Are you measuring the right indicators in your team? How often do you review these metrics in a way that encourages collaboration and continuous improvement?
5. **Feedback and Growth**
   When was the last time you sought candid feedback on your leadership style? How did you respond, and what changes did you implement?
6. **Personal Experiences**
   Which life events have most shaped your leadership philosophy? Have you shared these lessons openly with your team to foster transparency and trust?

Reflecting on these questions is already a step toward embodying the synergy of **head** and **heart**. When organizations yearn for innovation and resiliency, a savvy culture leader emerges as a beacon of possibility. By weaving empathy and accountability together, you can create a workplace where employees thrive, families benefit, and communities feel the ripple effect of purposeful intention leadership.

About the Author

Mildred Black

Founder of People Optimum Consulting, Transformation Coach, Speaker, Lecturer, Storyteller, & Author

Mildred Black, MBA, SHRM-SCP, is widely recognized for her pioneering work at the intersection of people and culture. As an expert in organizational consulting and human resources, she specializes in designing and implementing people-centered transformations, leadership development initiatives, and facilitated learning experiences. Her passion lies in aligning strategy, workplace culture, and professional growth to unlock human potential, fostering environments where individuals and organizations thrive.

Mildred is the founder of *People Optimum Consulting*, a firm that partners with clients ranging from entrepreneurial ventures to Fortune 100 companies like Amazon and Mercedes-Benz. Through their *Organizational Performance Optimization System™*, Mildred and her team engage leaders in establishing a robust culture foundation, building accountability, aligning strategic priorities, and cultivating a vibrant organizational environment. In addition, *The Optimize Academy* provides transformative learning experiences and coaching for leaders, entrepreneurs, and intrapreneurs, empowering them to positively impact the world around them.

Beyond her consulting work, Mildred is **co-author of the Amazon bestseller *Speaking My Truth*** and author of ***The Being Journal***. A sought-after *transformation coach, speaker, lecturer,* and *storyteller*, she has addressed audiences both nationally and internationally. She is also a media contributor whose thought leadership has been featured in *The Wall Street Journal*, *ABC*, and *Fox News*. Recognized by *The Wall Street Journal* as a Diversity+Business expert, she launched the *People+Culture Vodcast* and writes the *People+Culture Newsletter* on LinkedIn, igniting dialogue around today's most pressing workplace challenges and solutions.

Mildred earned her Executive MBA in Business Leadership from Georgia State University and a Bachelor of Science in Business Administration with a concentration in Finance from The University of Alabama. She further enriched her global perspective by studying business practices in Shanghai and Beijing, China, and strategy at

Harvard Extension School. In addition, she holds a Senior Human Resources Professional certification from both the Society for Human Resources Management and the Human Resources Certification Institute.

Deeply committed to service, Mildred is driven by a desire to create pathways for growth, development, and healing from the negative impacts of systemic trauma and poverty. Her volunteerism and community leadership focus on broadening opportunities for individuals and businesses from underrepresented backgrounds. Fueled by her belief in education, creativity, and synergy, Mildred strives to spark positive change in organizations, communities, and the people who shape them.

Contact Information

Email: https://peopleoptimum.com
Website: mildred@peopleotimum.com
Social Media:
https://linkedIn.com/in/iammildredblack
https://instagram.com/iammildredblack
https://facebook/iammildredblack

PERFORMANCE

ELEVATING IMPACT WITHOUT BURNOUT

Performance in leadership is not about relentless effort, it is about intentionality, sustainability, and purpose-driven impact. True success is not defined by exhaustion but by the ability to drive meaningful results while maintaining energy, focus, and overall well-being. The most effective leaders do not simply execute tasks; they align their efforts with a greater vision, ensuring their contributions command recognition and propel them forward. Controlling your performance narrative is about strategically showcasing your impact and positioning yourself for leadership opportunities rather than waiting to be noticed.

To redefine leadership, we must abandon the outdated belief that success is a product of overwork and instead embrace a model that values strategic execution, efficiency, and long-term influence. The leaders who rise are not those who do the most; they are those who deliver the highest value, cultivate purpose in their work, and inspire teams to achieve more with clarity and direction. In the chapters ahead, our authors redefine high performance—not as an endless pursuit of more but as optimal performance, purpose-driven leadership, and the art of making every move count.

Chapter 4

Owning Your Performance Narrative

Your Work Speaks for Itself; Make Sure It's Heard

Kristin Bell, SPHR

Are you the protagonist in your story or are you a background character in someone else's version of it?

We often hear that there are three sides to every story: your side, "their" side, and the truth existing somewhere in between. The reality is that the "truth" becomes what people believe based on the information available and how they feel about you. The way your story is shared matters a great deal on what becomes the "truth".

Early in my career as an HR practitioner, I fell in love with recruiting and talent acquisition. I joined nearly 100 groups through Facebook, LinkedIn, Meetup, professional organizations, local events, you name it. Helping others secure opportunities was natural for me and I quickly became the "go-to" person in my hometown and among former classmates. Something about knowing that I played an active role in advocating for someone to fill a position that not only added value to the organization but would be life-changing for that person and their family brought joy to my heart. I could feel light radiating from my spirit in those moments.

In one of my early talent roles, I was managing requisitions that had high volumes of internal applicants. For some, it was the desire to transition from a frontline, customer service position to a more professional, corporate role. These employees knew that the physical work environment and compensation that existed on the "other side" would change the trajectory of their careers and lifestyles. Yet, there was so much stigma about employees who continuously applied for internal roles (which they were qualified for) and continued to be passed over. While part of this was due to personal biases from hiring managers (and HR employees), the image and exposure of those employees also played a significant role in the weight of their actual performance. So, who is telling your story? Is it you? Is it your current manager? Is it someone else who works closely with you?

In Harvey J. Coleman's P.I.E. success theory, performance only accounted for 10% of the pie. So why spend so much time talking about such a small fraction? It's because this is the part we have to get right to have a chance at building a solid image and exposure. And if we're not strategic about it, it impacts our mental health, our confidence, our relationships, our future opportunities, and our money. It is common to focus on what you need to do to land a new position (internally and externally).

Redefining leadership and owning your performance narrative are deeply interconnected because modern leadership requires breaking away from traditional, one-size-fits-all models of success and embracing authentic, proactive storytelling about your contributions and potential. It shifts the focus toward individuality, resilience, and authenticity. While acknowledging systemic biases, owning your performance narrative combats barriers by ensuring your achievements and potential aren't overlooked or misinterpreted. You claim the power to articulate your unique strengths and redefine how their value is perceived. Leadership is as much about perception as it is about execution. When you take control of your performance story, you redefine what leadership looks like in your workplace or industry and normalize diverse approaches to leadership.

While your work may speak for itself, is it heard? Has your work ever lost its identity? In this chapter, we will explore the core elements of performance and how to establish systems of success that give your work a voice and portray you as a leader in an authentic way.

The Pitfalls of Performing Unprepared

Several years ago, I made what I thought was a pivotal and exciting move in my career. Burnt out as the only Black person in my HR department, I leapt at an offer from a well-known HR technology company that promised a fresh start. It wasn't just a new role, it was a new beginning. As a program manager, I relocated to South Florida with big dreams of reimagining inclusive hiring strategies and fostering belonging within an organization that needed a blank canvas for change. What I found was the opportunity to co-create the company's first race-based Employee Resource Group (ERG), BUILD (Black Ultipeeps in Leadership and Development). I finally felt seen, heard, and valued. My new manager trusted me, my colleagues treated me like family, and I believed I was doing meaningful work.

For the first time, I felt I was part of something transformative.

Then the pandemic hit, and with it came the racial unrest that rocked the nation in 2020. May 25, 2020, was a day that forever changed me, and millions of others, as we witnessed the horrifying death of George Floyd. As a DEI leader and the co-chair of BUILD, I felt the weight of my team's grief and pain and knew I needed to act. I sent a message to our talent acquisition team acknowledging the events, offering words of encouragement, and sharing resources to support them. In that moment, I felt strong, empowered, and deeply connected to my role as a leader. It wasn't just about my job; it was about doing what felt like a basic human responsibility, offering support in a time of crisis and making sure my people knew they were seen.

What I didn't anticipate, however, was the backlash.

Shortly after, I found myself in a meeting with the newly merged company's VP of Talent Acquisition, who questioned why I sent the email without her approval. Her reaction floored me. I had acted in the team's best interest, responding to a moment of racial trauma with empathy and support. But instead of acknowledging the urgency and compassion of my decision, she seemed to be more concerned about why I hadn't run it by her first, as though I had overstepped my bounds. It felt like she was trying to "check" me, as if I had done something wrong by speaking up when, in my view, I had done the right thing. I was annoyed- annoyed that she was questioning my judgment, annoyed that I had to explain myself, and annoyed by the underlying power dynamics at play. Her timid approach to the conversation made it worse, almost as if she was unsure how to engage with me on the subject, an unspoken discomfort that only deepened my frustration.

But even more telling was the response I received from the rest of the team. They were grateful. They felt seen. They thanked me for acknowledging their pain and creating space for the conversation that so many others had avoided. They were relieved to know that a leader on the team cared enough to speak out. And yet, in contrast, I could feel the unease of the white leadership from the Kronos team. They were a predominantly white group with no Black employees, and I could sense that my email had made them uncomfortable, perhaps even challenged the status quo in a way they weren't ready for. How telling it was that I, as a Black woman, was the one to take this step while they hesitated to acknowledge the humanity of my people.

My rebuttal, calm but firm, seemed to unnerve her. That meeting marked the beginning of a tense dynamic, one where I was constantly reminded of my identity, my position, and the bias that seeped into every interaction. It culminated in her delivering a performance review with vague feedback and biased language that painted me as "defensive," without examples or context to support it. That feedback, though baseless, became a weapon to undermine my credibility and jeopardize my future opportunities within the organization.

I had been working passionately and tirelessly, yet I was *performing unprepared.* I had not documented my contributions, articulated my value, or shaped the narrative of my work. Instead, I relied on the impact of my efforts to speak for itself. I didn't manage up, didn't establish clear expectations, and didn't build the relationships that could have shielded me when biases surfaced. In essence, I failed to own my performance narrative, and it cost me.

Reflecting on this experience, I see clearly how these pitfalls hindered not only my ability to advocate for myself but also my opportunity to redefine leadership in that space. Leadership isn't just about doing great work; it's about ensuring others see and value that work. It's about communicating with emotional intelligence, building cross-functional relationships, and creating a framework where your achievements align with the organization's goals.

Ultimately, I left the organization and filed an EEOC claim, but the real growth came in the lessons I learned. Performing unprepared taught me the importance of owning my narrative, documenting my achievements, and advocating for my value unapologetically. This experience fueled my passion for empowering others, especially Black women, to take up space, own their stories, and challenge leadership norms. It's not enough to perform; we must redefine what leadership looks like starting with ourselves.

The Fundamentals and Purpose of Performance Management

Let's start with the core elements of performance management. There are common misconceptions and perspectives on its purpose and effectiveness. Performance management isn't just a process; it's a strategic and dynamic opportunity to align individual and team contributions with an organization's broader goals. By grounding yourself in these elements, you create a foundation that drives meaningful results and long-term impact. There are four core elements we can consider when thinking about performance: *goal setting, feedback, development, and monitoring.*

Goal Setting: Connecting Vision to Action

Within the context of performance management, the process of identifying means understanding where you are today, where you want to be in the future, and what needs to happen in between to get there. Goal setting is the process of identifying and establishing clear, specific, and measurable objectives that an individual or organization aims to achieve within a certain time frame. It is a fundamental aspect of planning, both in personal development and professional environments, and serves as a roadmap for achieving desired outcomes.

The connection between effort and outcome strengthens the story of the value of your achievements and contributions. Setting goals gives you ownership over your performance and development. Goals allow you to translate your vision into action in a way that others can see and understand. They connect where you've been to where you're going, ensuring that your performance narrative reflects your impact and your legacy as a leader.

Feedback: The Foundation for Growth

Feedback is often described as positive or negative. Feedback is a transformative tool that shapes your ability to adapt, improve, and excel. It's not just about receiving praise or criticism, it's about gaining actionable insights that reinforce strengths and redirect behaviors when necessary. Feedback builds self-awareness and emotional intelligence, both essential for effective leadership. It reflects how others experience your work and illuminate opportunities for growth. When you actively seek and apply feedback, you foster trust, collaboration, and a culture of continuous improvement. Feedback isn't just a checkpoint; it's a mechanism for refining your performance narrative and amplifying your influence.

Development: Leading Through Growth

Development is the deliberate process of acquiring and refining skills and knowledge on the journey of growth to being better and preparing for future opportunities. It provides the skills, confidence, and adaptability needed to craft a compelling story of value and progress while inspiring others to do the same. By committing to growth, you position yourself as a leader and show that your journey is ongoing and that your leadership is defined by evolution, not stagnation or a single moment in time. In essence, development allows you to lead not just by what you do but by how you grow.

Monitoring: Driving Results with Precision

Monitoring the ongoing process of tracking and assessing results against outcomes and observing key performance indicators. It ensures accountability, clarity, and the ability to course correct in real time. Monitoring is the engine that drives ownership of your performance narrative and redefines leadership as a dynamic and results-driven process. By tracking your progress, aligning with goals, and making real-time adjustments, you ensure that your story is one of intentionality, growth, and measurable impact. It ensures that both your narrative and your leadership are always grounded in evidence, progress, and purpose.

These four core elements provide a framework for redefining leadership as intentional, adaptable, and purpose-driven. Mastering these fundamentals sets the stage for sustained growth, more profound influence, and transformational impact. Your performance narrative becomes a testament to your ability to balance vision with action, resilience with adaptability, and leadership with authenticity.

Owning Your Performance Narrative

First, what is a performance narrative? A performance narrative describes your work performance, contributions, and achievements over a specific period, as equally important, how others experience you. It provides a way for you to frame your experiences, highlight your successes, address challenges, and demonstrate how your efforts align with the organization's goals while sharing "what's next" for you. It's more than just meeting or exceeding expectations in your work, it's about your image, your brand, your exposure and how this is communicated to others. To own your performance narrative means that you influence "what's next" and shape the perceptions of how others experience you.

Too often, we fall into myths about performance:

- **Myth #1:** "If I work hard, my contributions will speak for themselves."
  Reality: Hard work is important, but visibility is key. If no one knows the value you bring, your efforts may go unnoticed.
- **Myth #2:** "Acknowledging challenges shows weakness."
  Reality: Addressing challenges and solutions demonstrates resilience, adaptability, and the courage to grow.
- **Myth #3:** "A performance review is the only time to showcase your narrative."
  Reality: Every interaction is an opportunity to influence how others perceive you.

A strong performance narrative has six key components that work together to tell a compelling story:

1. **Achievements and Contributions:** Highlight projects, innovations, leadership roles, and problem-solving efforts that positively impacted the organization.
2. **Alignment with Goals:** Show how your work connects to broader organizational objectives, reinforcing your value as a strategic contributor.
3. **Challenges and Solutions:** Don't shy away from obstacles you've faced. Share how you overcame them to demonstrate resilience and creativity.
4. **Growth and Development:** Acknowledge areas for improvement and how you're proactively growing. Self-awareness and evolution show leadership maturity.
5. **Future Goals:** Paint a picture of what's next, how you plan to continue driving success and impact.
6. **Supporting Evidence:** Use metrics, feedback, and specific examples to ground your narrative in undeniable facts.

There are numerous opportunities, both formal and informal, to share your performance narrative, ensuring your contributions and impact are visible to the right audience. Your narrative isn't confined to a performance review. It's a living, breathing story you can share in many ways:

- **LinkedIn Posts:** Go beyond job descriptions listing tasks or activities. Highlight your measurable impact, lessons learned, and areas of development.
- **Podcasts or Webinars:** This is a creative avenue to build a personal brand, share your expertise and

insights to build credibility and expand your influence to a broader audience.
- **Newsletters or Portfolios:** Create regular updates showcasing your progress and contributions to stakeholders, mentors, or peers within your organization. This method is a career differentiator and game changer.
- **Skip-Level Meetings:** Use these opportunities to align your efforts with organizational priorities while showcasing your value.
- **Performance Review:** a critical moment to deliver your narrative with clarity and confidence, especially as it often influences compensation and promotions.

Beyond these, unique options could include internal webinars, blogging on professional platforms, or even participating in panel discussions, all of which allow you to share your story and amplify your presence both within and beyond your organization.

When Your Performance is Questioned

Even the strongest narrative can be challenged. The real question is: Are you ready to advocate for yourself? Do you have evidence to back up your contributions? When your performance is questioned, it's not a time to panic; it's a moment to stand firm, lean into your story, and own the value you bring.

Why Owning Your Narrative Matters

Your performance narrative shapes your professional identity. It ensures that your contributions aren't just recognized; they're remembered. It's your way of influencing what comes next, crafting a legacy, and showing that leadership is about more than just hitting goals. It's about building trust, inspiring growth, and making an impact that resonates beyond the workplace.

Your Work Speaks For Itself; Make Sure It's Heard

To start owning your performance narrative today and redefining leadership through intentional action, focus on building relationships, leveraging others to amplify your work, and ensuring your contributions remain distinctly yours. Begin by setting clear, actionable goals: schedule a conversation with your manager to align on role expectations and establish short-term (30, 60, 90 days) and long-term objectives. Document these goals in a performance tracking tool or system to ensure easy reference and track your progress over time.

Next, create a habit of systemizing feedback loops by scheduling regular one-on-one meetings with your manager or key stakeholders. Use these opportunities to discuss your progress, gather constructive feedback, and align your narrative with organizational priorities. Leaders who embrace feedback and goal setting demonstrate intentionality and adaptability, core traits of redefined leadership. Working in isolation can open the door for your work to lose its identity and your contribution to the bottom line.

Relationships are central to amplifying your work. Build connections across teams, departments, and external networks. Engage others to champion your efforts while maintaining clear ownership of your contributions. Collaboration amplifies your impact, but transparency ensures your narrative stays authentic and distinctly yours.

Additionally, start tracking your achievements and contributions in real time. Use a journal, digital tool, or app to log key successes, including outcomes, challenges overcome, and the impact of your work. Summarize these into monthly or quarterly updates to share with stakeholders via newsletters, team meetings, or skip-level presentations. Sharing your progress highlights your ability to deliver results and inspires others to do the same.

Externally, redefine leadership by extending your narrative to broader audiences. Use platforms like LinkedIn to showcase your expertise, celebrate milestones, and connect with industry peers. Participate in podcasts, webinars, or panel discussions to amplify your personal brand and demonstrate the power of authentic leadership. By actively sharing your performance narrative both internally and externally, you challenge traditional notions of leadership and show that influence stems from transparency, intentionality, and the ability to connect with others through your story.

Your performance narrative is your power, it reflects your skills, resilience, and the leadership potential only you can embody. By taking control of your story, you redefine leadership as something deeply personal yet universally impactful. Leadership isn't just about titles or authority; it's about how you articulate your contributions, navigate challenges, and inspire others through your actions. Speak up, document your achievements, and proactively showcase your value, because true leadership starts with owning your narrative.

As you move forward, ask yourself: *Am I performing with intention, or am I risking the pitfalls of performing unprepared?* Your performance narrative is the bridge between your contributions and the leadership legacy you're building. Own it boldly, leverage relationships strategically, and redefine how leadership looks and feels in the spaces you occupy.

Conclusion

As you move forward in your career, remember that you have the power to define your story and shape how your achievements are seen and valued. Owning your performance narrative is about standing firmly in your accomplishments and expressing your contributions with clarity and confidence. For women, especially Black women, navigating the various spaces where we're often underrepresented, this can be a powerful tool for gaining the recognition we deserve. Embrace every moment, every milestone, and every challenge as part of your unique and invaluable journey.

Your performance narrative reflects your skills, resilience, and the impact you make, so don't let it be shaped by anyone else. Take control of your story by actively documenting and sharing your achievements. Each success, big or small, contributes to the larger picture of who you are and the value you bring. Make it a habit to regularly reflect on your progress and understand the breadth of your work. This not only builds confidence but also serves as a reminder of your strengths when you face obstacles.

Building this narrative also means advocating for yourself. Speak up about the work you're doing, ask for feedback, and be vocal about the goals you want to achieve. Don't wait for someone else to acknowledge your contributions; be proactive in showcasing the value you add. When you own your narrative, you define how others perceive your growth, potential, and ambition.

Remember that your journey is uniquely yours, and it's okay if it doesn't look like anyone else's. Own the experiences and qualities that make you who you are and let them inform your narrative. Each step you take and each achievement you celebrate is part of a story that only you can tell. When you embrace this story and share it authentically, you inspire others to do the same.

So, as you lead, grow, and make your mark, know that you are already creating a legacy. Owning your performance narrative is a continuous journey of self-advocacy, growth, and resilience. Keep pushing forward, and let your story shine as a testament to your strength, skill, and the path you're blazing for those who come after you.

About the Author

Kristin Bell, SPHR

HR Innovator | Equity Advocate | Tech Entrepreneur

Hailing from Little Rock, Arkansas, Kristin Bell has built a career at the crossroads of innovation, equity, and leadership. With a Bachelor's degree in Finance from Henderson State University and HRCI-SPHR certification, Kristin brings over a decade of diverse experience spanning higher education, healthcare, finance, technology, and manufacturing. Her multifaceted expertise encompasses talent acquisition, employee relations, HR operations, strategy, DEI, and talent management, all driven by her mission to disrupt traditional systems and create meaningful opportunities for all.

In 2023, Kristin cemented her reputation as a trailblazer by co-founding two visionary ventures. As a co-founder of **ReviewTailor**, a Techstars Portfolio Company, she is revolutionizing HR performance management with AI-powered tools that promote fairness and employee growth. Simultaneously, she launched **CultureCite**, an empowering app designed to help employees stand against workplace retaliation, discrimination, and harassment. These groundbreaking platforms are a testament to Kristin's ability to turn ideas into impactful solutions that redefine the workplace.

As Managing Partner of **CEEID HR Consulting, LLC**, Kristin collaborates with organizations to transform their HR strategies. She serves as a trusted advisor in performance management, talent acquisition, DEI, leadership development, and organizational strategy, consistently delivering innovative approaches to complex challenges.

A recognized thought leader and co-author of *Leadership Redefined*, Kristin inspires others with her chapter on owning your performance narrative. Her insights empower readers to embrace self-awareness, take charge of their professional growth, and break through barriers to success.

Currently residing in Atlanta, Georgia, Kristin balances her professional life with a vibrant array of passions. From uncovering hidden gems in her city to traveling, golfing, painting, wine tasting, and staying active, she embodies the belief that a fulfilled life fuels a thriving career.

Kristin Bell is a force for change, a voice for equity, and an innovator who transforms bold ideas into solutions that make workplaces and the world more inclusive, empowering, and just.

Contact Information

Website: www.reviewtailor.com
LinkedIn: https://www.linkedin.com/in/kristinlbell/

Chapter 5

Redefining Executive Leadership Through Health and Wellbeing

Being Healthy and Successful Looks Good on You

Dr. Alicia Newsome

What if pushing through exhaustion wasn't the key to success but the very thing keeping you from it?

We've all heard the rallying cries for high performance: push harder, do more, sleep less, and outwork the competition. It's a pervasive narrative that it's become a badge of honor to teeter on the edge of burnout, all in the name of titles, performance, results, leadership, and ultimately, success. But what if we've been chasing the wrong goal? What if the answer isn't high performance as we know it, but something deeper: *optimal performance*? Not the exhausting grind, but the sustainable balance where energy, focus, and well-being align to unlock true success.

It was a typical Sunday afternoon. I was curled up, fast asleep on the couch at a friend's house. Sundays after church were a ritual, kids running in and out of the house, their laughter echoing through the rooms, and the unmistakable smell of a good Sunday meal cooking in the kitchen. While life was happening all around me, my friends had come to expect this scene: me on the couch, tucked under a blanket, sound asleep.

At that point in my life, exhaustion was my constant companion. I had two little girls, just two and three years old, navigating a painful divorce and simultaneously managing my wellness practice. I was running on empty, relying on adrenaline, prayer, and caffeine to get me through the days.

Evenings were no better; after picking up my kids from daycare, my singular focus was getting them into bed so I could collapse into sleep myself. There was no energy left for friends, family, or even myself.

Does this sound familiar? Have you ever reached a point in life where sleep felt like your only refuge?

A long list of tasks waits for you, but your body simply won't cooperate. It's midday, and you find yourself craving a nap or needing your afternoon coffee before the next meeting. It's early evening, and instead of unwinding or connecting with loved ones, you're dozing off on the couch. Maybe you've dragged yourself to your children's events, struggling to stay present, or relied on your morning coffee and mid-afternoon pick-me-ups just to keep going.

I've been there. I know how it feels to be exhausted yet expected to perform, to give so much to everyone else while leaving nothing for yourself. If you're experiencing this right now, you are not alone.

For over a decade, I've worked with men and women in corporate events, retreats, courses, and exclusive VIP settings, helping them *look better, feel better,* and ultimately *perform better*. But here's the truth: life isn't just about how much we can accomplish or produce. It's about leading a healthy, vibrant life so that we can show up for the people who need us most, our children, our partners, our friends, our teams, our clients, and our communities. These people count on us to be present, energetic, and focused. They deserve our best. But how can we offer that if we're running on empty, worn down, and dare I say it, burned out?

I know this struggle firsthand. Every Sunday afternoon when I was asleep on that couch, I was overwhelmed with guilt. I *needed* the rest, but I couldn't escape the pressure I put on myself. I felt like I was failing my kids, unable to give them the attention they craved and deserved. I wanted to be the mom who was fully engaged, volunteering for field trips, baking homemade desserts, and bringing games and prizes to school parties. And in some ways, I did all of that. But I did it through gritted teeth, begrudgingly pushing through exhaustion and sometimes with resentment because I had so many other things to do. But I still got it done.

The truth was, I had learned to function through my burnout. I became what I call *high-functioning burnout.* On the outside, I was still showing up, "getting it done," and checking the boxes. But on the inside, I was paying a heavy price. I was chronically fatigued, plagued with neck and back pain, digestion issues, awful hormonal imbalances, and relentless brain fog.

In our society, exhaustion, brain fog, fatigue, bloating, stress, overwhelm, and hormonal imbalances have become *normalized*. These symptoms are so common that many women dismiss them as part of life's demands, something to "push through." I saw this play out firsthand during a corporate workshop I was leading for senior executives.

After my session, a woman approached me, an accomplished leader overseeing a large team and managing high-stakes projects. She shared that she was "doing fine" health-wise but wanted "a little more energy" to help her keep up with her demanding schedule. As we continued talking, her story began to unravel. She described needing *three cups of coffee* just to get through her morning meetings, often skipping lunch because she was too busy, and finding herself drained and asleep on the couch by 7:30 p.m., long before her kids went to bed.

What struck me most was when she casually mentioned her monthly migraines. Every month, like clockwork, she'd experience crippling headaches that forced her to cancel meetings, reschedule presentations, or push through with pain medication, often at the expense of her performance and focus. Yet she brushed it off as *"just part of being a woman."*

There she is, a high-performing leader, respected, accomplished, and driven, who thought it was "normal" to rely on caffeine, push through pain, and crash early, month after month. She didn't recognize that these symptoms were red flags her body was waving, signaling imbalance and burnout.

This mindset is all too common. In leadership circles, we praise resilience and reward output. But when we normalize dysfunction, we compromise not only our health but also our ability to lead, innovate, and thrive. We can't be our sharpest in the boardroom if we're running on fumes. We can't bring our best ideas to the table if our brains are clouded by fatigue or migraines.

The truth is, the symptoms we brush off as *common*, like chronic headaches, exhaustion, or irregular cycles, are far from normal. For women in leadership, optimal performance requires more than grit and caffeine. It demands a body and mind that are aligned, energized, and thriving. True performance isn't about pushing harder, it's about honoring your body, harnessing your energy, and thriving in a way that not only sustains you but also elevates your ability to inspire, influence, and lead effectively.

The Wake-Up Call

Seeing the health crisis unfold firsthand, both in and outside of my virtual clinic, has deepened my passion for helping people wake up and take control of their health journey. The numbers don't lie, and the statistics are staggering. It's time to confront the reality of our nation's health epidemic.

- According to the American Cancer Society, *one in three people* will be diagnosed with cancer, and *one in three* will die from it.
- The American Diabetes Association reports that *one in three* American adults are prediabetic, yet *84% of them have no idea*.
- The American Heart Association reveals that *half* of all heart attacks occur with no prior warning, and for

the other half, the warning signs often go unrecognized. Tragically, *50% of people who have a heart attack* die from it.

At a time when *Alzheimer's, diabetes, cancer,* and *heart disease* are skyrocketing, these statistics are not just numbers, they belong to *us*. If we don't take action, we risk becoming part of these devastating trends.

We are living in a time when the health of our families, colleagues, and communities is under siege. These realities demand our attention and action. If we do not prioritize prevention, we risk becoming a statistic ourselves.

The Ripple Effect: Impact of Health on Optimal Performance

The woman I was on that Sunday afternoon, a leader struggling to keep her eyes open, missing out on precious moments with loved ones, wasn't living up to her full potential. And here's the truth: when leaders sacrifice their health, it impacts *everything*.

1. **Leaders Modeling Wellness:** When you prioritize your well-being, you don't just feel better, you *lead better*. You inspire your team to value their own health, fostering a culture where balance and performance coexist. Your example creates a ripple effect of trust, morale, and resilience within your organization.

2. **Fostering a Culture of Optimal Performance:** When health becomes a priority, productivity and engagement soar. Teams thrive when their leaders bring clarity, energy, and focus to the table. Leaders who model wellness set the standard for sustainable success, one that empowers the entire organization to perform at its best.

At the time, I didn't know how to listen to it or what to do about it. I was *functioning*, but I wasn't *thriving*. Like many women, I tried to push through, ignoring the signals my body was desperately sending me.

Hormones: The Foundation of Leading and Living Well

We all strive to show up as our best selves, whether in the boardroom, at home with our families, or pursuing personal goals. But let's face it: when your energy is drained, your focus is scattered, and your body feels out of sync, it's impossible to lead effectively. True leadership begins with self-leadership, and that includes cultivating sustainable practices that support your health as the foundation of your success.

I've been there, searching for answers in a sea of conflicting advice, from online articles to well-meaning friends, to "Dr. Google", Facebook groups, and even doctors who dismiss our concerns with a generic "everything looks normal." The frustration of knowing something is off but not finding solutions can leave you feeling unheard, stuck, and questioning yourself.

As a functional medicine doctor, that's why I created the RESET Framework. It's not about chasing quick fixes or perfection; it's about building a sustainable foundation for energy, focus, and vitality so you can thrive in every area of your life.

Hormones are the unsung heroes of this process. The number one reason your hormones are out of balance is that they need to be *reset*. These chemical messengers fuel energy, stabilize mood, enhance focus, and support physical beauty, think glowing skin, healthy hair, and the ability to maintain comfortable and enjoyable weight. They also impact how you think, feel, and perform, whether you're making decisions at work, managing relationships, or tackling personal goals. When your hormones are in sync, they fuel energy, sharpen focus, and stabilize mood, allowing you to show up as the leader your team, family, and community need. But when they're out of sync, even the most determined efforts can feel like an uphill battle. Fatigue clouds your judgment, brain fog stifles innovation, and mood swings can make it harder to connect authentically with others.

Sustainability is the answer, not just for your health but for your professional career. A sustainable approach means prioritizing practices that keep your body and mind aligned over the long term, giving you the resilience to lead with clarity and effectiveness, no matter what challenges arise. By focusing on hormone balance now, you're building a foundation for vibrant health, stress resiliency, and long-term well-being.

Imagine yourself 20 years from now. Will you have the energy to make decisions that shape the future of your organization? The stamina to mentor rising leaders? The vitality to innovate and drive meaningful change? By focusing on sustainability now, you're not just enhancing your performance today, you're securing your ability to lead powerfully into the future. Think about the simple joys of life. Will you have the energy to climb stairs, hike your favorite trails, or chase after grandkids? Will you still be able to travel freely, enjoy vacations, or live life without being limited by health concerns?

Think of resetting your hormones like rebooting your body's operating system. Imagine a computer that's running slow, glitching, or crashing because too many programs are running in the background. Stress, poor sleep, environmental toxins, and dietary habits do the same thing to your hormones, they overwhelm your system, leaving you fatigued, foggy, moody, and out of sync.

When you hit *reset* on a computer, you clear out the unnecessary clutter and restore its efficiency, bringing it back to how it was designed to run. Resetting your hormones does the same thing. It clears out the "noise" and disruptors, recalibrating your body to its natural state so everything can run smoothly again. This isn't about work-life balance; it's about operating sustainably to support energy, focus, and vitality in the long term.

But the RESET Framework goes beyond a simple reboot. It's about addressing the root causes of hormonal overload and achieving a true "factory reset." The goal is to restore your body to its *optimal state*: healthy, energized, and ready to perform at your best. When your body is aligned, your leadership transforms. You make better decisions, solve problems with creativity and innovation, and connect more deeply with your team. You lead not from a place of depletion but from a well of sustainable energy that fuels your effectiveness at work and your presence in life.

This isn't about perfection. It's about creating a sustainable foundation for balance, so your body can handle life's demands without constantly running into "glitches." Resetting your hormones means starting fresh, building resilience, and preparing your health for whatever challenges life brings next.

The RESET Framework

The RESET Framework is built on *Four Pillars*, the foundation for achieving balanced hormones and vibrant health:

1. **Pillar One:** Identify the root cause of your symptoms and stress.
2. **Pillar Two:** Choose to test, not guess.
3. **Pillar Three:** Boost your metabolism and detox properly.

4. **Pillar Four:** Prioritize your well-being and protect your future.

Key Truth: Resetting your hormones brings balance to your body and your life.

So, how do you get started? Below, I outline five steps to help you implement the **Four Pillars** and begin your journey toward hormonal balance.

Step 1: Evaluate your symptoms and their impact on your life.

The first step to resetting your hormones and reclaiming your health is to listen to your body and assess how your symptoms are affecting your life. Just as an effective leader evaluates a team's strengths and weaknesses to optimize performance, you need to take an honest inventory of your health to identify imbalances and their broader effects on your relationships, career, and overall quality of life.

Start by keeping a health journal. Track your symptoms with specifics, what you're experiencing (e.g., fatigue, bloating, mood swings, headaches), when it happens (time of day, week, or month), potential triggers (diet, stress, sleep), and how it impacts your daily life (e.g., missing deadlines, feeling short-tempered, avoiding social events). Over time, patterns will emerge that can offer insights into the root causes of your symptoms.

Take time to reflect on the ripple effect of these symptoms. Are they affecting your ability to focus at work, lead effectively, or connect with your family? Have they diminished your confidence or caused you to withdraw from activities you once loved? Acknowledging the real-life impact of these issues creates clarity and motivation to take action and seek solutions.

It's also important to assess what you've already tried to address your symptoms. Have you relied on over-the-counter remedies, supplements, or quick fixes that only mask the problem? How much time, energy, and money have you spent searching for answers? This step helps you identify where you've been using band-aid solutions instead of addressing the deeper issues, preparing you for the clarity and solutions offered in later steps.

Finally, trust your intuition. Women are often conditioned to dismiss their instincts, especially when symptoms are minimized or explained away by others. If something feels off in your body, believe it. Your symptoms are valid, and your body is sending you signals that shouldn't be ignored. Evaluating them isn't about creating fear; it's about empowering yourself with awareness and taking back control of your health.

Step 2: Fully commit to uncovering the root cause of your symptoms.

Evaluating your symptoms is the first step in understanding the signals your body is sending you. But awareness alone isn't enough. To truly transform your health and reset your body, you must take the next bold step: commit fully to uncovering the root cause of your symptoms.

I love using the analogy of the check engine light in a car. When the light comes on, it's a clear signal that something needs attention, it's time for a maintenance check. Makes sense, right? So, imagine this:

You drive to the dealership and tell the mechanic the check engine light just came on. You mention that the car has been jerking a little, but otherwise, you haven't noticed much else. The mechanic jots down your concerns, asks you to take a seat, and ten minutes later, comes back with a sticker. He says, *"Here's what we recommend, just place this sticker right over the check engine light. People love our stickers; they have motivational quotes on them and make you feel good. That's all you need to do, just cover it up and don't worry about it anymore."*

If that really happened, you'd be outraged. You'd demand to speak to a manager, insist on a refund, and say, *"Why are we ignoring the light? You didn't even run diagnostics or look under the hood!"* We would never accept masking the problem with a sticker while the car's engine goes unchecked.

And yet, we allow this to happen to our health.

Doctors often "cover up" symptoms with quick fixes, medications, temporary remedies, or even some supplements, without investigating the root cause. I know this because I've seen it time and time again with my patients and clients. And I've been a victim of it myself.

If you're reading this, your body's check engine light may already be on. Symptoms like fatigue, brain fog, digestive issues, poor sleep, irritability, or thinning hair are not just inconveniences, they're signals. Your body is trying to tell you something. Intuitively, you may even sense that something feels "off." That's because it is.

You might already be taking steps to address your symptoms, perhaps using herbs or supplements. While these can be helpful tools, they aren't always the answer. I often explain it to my clients this way: imagine you have a headache. It's easy and convenient to reach for ibuprofen to make the pain go away. And yes, the headache disappears, but the question remains: *Why did you have the headache in the first place? It was not because your body was lacking ibuprofen. Something else is going on!*

Your body is speaking to you, don't silence it with a sticker. To truly feel better, function optimally, and regain vibrant health, you must "look under the hood." Symptoms are clues that deserve investigation, not masking.

Commitment is the cornerstone of reclaiming your health. This isn't about quick fixes; it's about fully investing your time, energy, and resources into uncovering the answers you deserve. This leads us to our next step.

Step 3: Get answers with root cause testing and comprehensive assessments.

This step is where science meets action, using root cause testing and comprehensive assessments to uncover the real reasons behind your symptoms.

For too long, women have been told their symptoms are "normal," only to feel dismissed when lab results come back "fine." Yet, fatigue, brain fog, bloating, weight gain, and hormonal disruptions persist. But "normal" isn't the same as optimal, and guessing, whether with diets, supplements, or trends, won't lead to lasting results. To truly reset your hormones and reclaim your energy, focus, and vitality, you need to test, not guess.

Fully committing to uncovering the root cause of your symptoms through root cause testing requires a shift in mindset. Insurance does not cover these types of advanced testing. And the tests run in the traditional medical system often come back "normal" for many women until they are given the awful diagnosis of diabetes, high cholesterol, high blood pressure, and even cancer.

Unlike standard lab tests that may only scratch the surface, root cause testing offers a deep dive into the systems that directly impact your energy, hormones, metabolism, and overall well-being. These tests provide a *complete picture* of what's happening inside your body. Root cause testing includes hormone testing, metabolic and nutrient testing, gut and digestive health assessments, and toxin and stress assessments.

Your health is an investment in your future. And you must recognize that your health is not an "extra" or something to address *when you have time*. It's the foundation of everything you do: your leadership, your relationships, your confidence, and your ability to thrive.

Step 4: Integrate nutrition and detox the right way, at the right time and in the right order.

After identifying symptoms and uncovering root causes, the next step is to restore balance through targeted nutrition and detoxification. These strategies are essential for resetting your hormones, boosting energy, and improving overall health, but here's the key: they must be done the *right way*, at the *right time,* and in the *right order.*

Quick fixes like juice cleanses or restrictive diets often backfire, leaving women feeling worse. Without proper preparation, detoxing can overwhelm your liver, kidneys, and digestive system, causing toxins to re-enter your bloodstream instead of being eliminated. Think of it like spring cleaning, if you don't prepare by clearing the clutter first, you'll just spread the mess around. You wouldn't start by vacuuming the floors if all the dust and clutter were still sitting on the countertops, right? You'd start by organizing, clearing out the mess, and preparing the space so you can clean thoroughly without spreading dirt around.

A structured, phased approach ensures your body is ready to detox safely and effectively. Using insights from root cause testing (Step 3), your detox and nutrition plan should be personalized to address your unique needs, like supporting liver function, reducing inflammation, or improving gut health.

Personalization ensures that detoxing and nutrition aren't a one-size-fits-all solution but rather a customized approach to help your body reset and thrive. This step is about clarity, not confusion. My role is to guide you through this process to eliminate the guesswork and ensure your body detoxes *safely* and *efficiently*.

Step 5: Surround yourself with support, accountability, and expert guidance.

The final step in the RESET Framework, and perhaps the most transformative, is to surround yourself with the *right* support, accountability, and expert guidance. This journey to resetting your hormones and reclaiming your health is not meant to be walked alone. The truth is, trying to "figure it all out" on your own can be exhausting, overwhelming, and counterproductive. Just as you lean on teams, mentors, and advisors in your career, you need a health support system that can guide you, hold you accountable, and help you stay on track.

For high-achieving, ambitious women, it's easy to take on everything alone. After all, you've built your success by pushing through challenges and relying on yourself. But when it comes to your health, isolation can stall progress. Here's why:

1. **Accountability Drives Results:** A supportive accountability partner, whether a health coach, root cause medicine doctor, or wellness group, ensures you stay committed to your goals, even when life gets busy or your motivation dips. Having someone to check in with, celebrate your wins, and gently redirect you when needed keeps you moving forward.

2. **Expert Guidance Provides Clarity:** Trying to "Google your way" to good health often leads to confusion and frustration. Experts bring years of training and experience to identify the root causes of your symptoms, design a personalized plan, and save you time, energy, and money by eliminating the guesswork.
3. **Support Creates Momentum:** Surrounding yourself with the right people, those who encourage you, share wisdom, and lift you up, keeps you inspired and motivated. You don't have to carry the weight of this journey alone.

Women in leadership know the power of collaboration, mentorship, and support in achieving success. The same principles apply to your health journey. Surrounding yourself with the right experts and accountability partners doesn't just make the process easier, it accelerates your results.

When you have people cheering you on, guiding you, and holding you to your commitments, you:

- Stay focused and motivated to follow through.
- Gain clarity and direction from expert insights.
- Build resilience for setbacks and celebrate progress along the way.

You were never meant to walk this journey alone. The truth is, no one reaches success without support, whether in health, business, or life. When I want to excel in any area of my life, I take one critical step: I hire a coach.

Whether it's for finances, business, spiritual development, or relationships, I seek out the best mentors, those who've been where I am, learned from their mistakes, and now have the wisdom to guide me forward. Why? Because success comes faster, easier, and with fewer missteps when you have someone knowledgeable in your corner.

The same applies to your health. Surround yourself with people who are qualified, experienced, and committed to seeing you thrive. Whether that's reading this book, asking for referrals, or taking a course, the key is to take the first step and invest in yourself.

Conclusion: Embracing Well-Being as the New Performance Standard

Sitting on that couch all those years ago, I didn't yet realize how critical my health was to every role I held, as a mother, a friend, a business owner, and a leader. I thought I was *doing enough* just by pushing through and getting things done, but the truth is, I was merely surviving with *high functioning burnout*. When I was falling asleep by 7 p.m., I couldn't be the mother I wanted to be, let alone the leader I was called to be. I had to prioritize daily habits that would help me sustain energy and focus, not just for one day, but every day.

Leadership today demands a shift. Success is no longer just about what you produce, it's about *how well you live and lead*. Prioritizing your health is the ultimate power move. When you feel your best, you *show up* as the powerhouse you're meant to be. Just as you protect your career milestones and deadlines, protecting your well-being must become non-negotiable.

Reflection Questions:

1. Is your body sending you "check engine light" signals right now? If so, what are they?
2. What's at stake if nothing changes? Will fatigue, brain fog, or stubborn weight continue to hold you back in your career or personal life?
3. Where will you be one year from now? Five years? Ten?
4. How will your health affect your relationships, career, and quality of life?
5. How would regaining balance in your health impact your leadership, team morale, and family?
6. Imagine yourself one year from now: What changes can you make *today* to begin thriving in every area of your life?

About the Author

Dr. Alicia Newsome

International Speaker | Best Selling Author Corporate Trainer | Functional Medicine Doctor & Founder of Powerful & Healthy Academy

Dr. Alicia Newsome is an acclaimed international speaker, 3x best-selling author, corporate trainer, and a distinguished doctor specializing in functional medicine. With a career spanning over 15 years, Dr. Alicia has transformed thousands of lives through her innovative approaches to women's health, captivating audiences and clients worldwide with her profound insights and actionable strategies.

Dr. Alicia is a sought-after authority, having conducted training and lectures at some of the world's most prestigious institutions, including Yale University, Mayo Clinic, Johns Hopkins, and Fortune 500 companies. Her expertise in functional medicine, human nutrition, and genetics uniquely positions her to uncover the root causes of complex health issues and guide individuals toward holistic, lasting solutions.

Recognized for her contributions to healthcare and empowerment, Dr. Alicia has been featured in *USA Today, ABC, NBC, FOX, CBS,* and *The Great Social Club* and is an honored recipient of the *United States Presidential Lifetime Achievement Award.* Her passion for addressing women's health challenges has led her to consult on high-profile clinical trials and specialize in conditions such as endometriosis, fibroids, and hormone imbalances, blending her expertise in both conventional and natural medicine.

As the visionary founder of **Powerful & Healthy Academy**, Dr. Alicia empowers women seeking clarity and direction to reclaim their authentic voices, transform their health, and boldly pursue their life purpose. Through her Reset Framework™, a proven, step-by-step approach, she helps women reset their hormones, regain their health, and completely change the trajectory of their lives. Her work extends globally through a well-respected supplement line, luxury health and wellness retreats, books, live events, digital courses, and *The Root Podcast,* where she delves into critical women's health topics.

Dr. Alicia's private practice offers boutique-style concierge care, including root-cause lab testing, VIP coaching, and customized group programs designed to meet the individual needs of each client. Her holistic and personalized approach ensures that women not only heal but also thrive in every aspect of their lives.

When not transforming lives, Dr. Alicia enjoys spending time with her husband and three children, hosting gourmet dinner parties, traveling to tropical destinations, and swimming. Her unwavering dedication to empowering women to ask the right questions, get accurate answers, and reclaim their health has made her a trusted leader and transformational force in functional medicine and beyond.

Contact Information:

Dr. Alicia Newsome
Website: www.dralicianewsome.com
Email: dralicia@dralicianewsome.com
Instagram: @dr.alicianewsome
Facebook: dralicianewsome
LinkedIn: https://www.linkedin.com/in/dr-alicia-newsome/
Supplements: www.rootcaresupplements.com

Chapter 6

The Journey and Lessons to Achieving Optimal Performance

Harnessing P.E.A.K. Purpose and Resilience to Overcome Adversity

Patrice Key

Adversity is not a barrier; it's a bridge. The question is, how will you cross it?

Turning Adversity into Strength

Little did I know, adversity was a part of life and one that I would experience continuously. I was born into humble beginnings, where poverty and hardship were constants. Homelessness, addiction, and the shadow of generational trauma stole my childhood, burdening me with struggles I hadn't chosen. My story seemed written before I could even find my voice. But despite the weight of these beginnings, I made a choice to forge a new path, break the chains of the past, and build the family I had always dreamed of.

In mid-2004, I found myself alone in Dallas, TX, pregnant with my first child. I hoped that this new chapter would signal an end to the hardships that had once defined my life, believing that a brighter future was finally within reach. My pregnancy felt like a promise, a new beginning. But at just 16 weeks, the dream shattered. I was in preterm labor, and no interventions could prevent it. My days blurred into a haze of pain, relentless medications, and procedures that drained me physically and emotionally. My body became a battleground of infections and exhaustion, a constant reminder of how fragile life could be. Yet even in the darkest moments, my baby fought to stay alive, her tiny foot pressing against my cervix, a fierce, determined signal of her will to survive.

Then, at 25 weeks, on the third day of the ninth month, my daughter came into this world at exactly 11:11 a.m. She weighed just 1 lb. 11 oz. In that moment, as I held this tiny, fragile life in my hands, I knew everything had changed. If there was ever a sign that hope could survive against the odds, she was it. My life's story had hit its turning point, and this was only the beginning of a journey that would redefine what was possible. That moment at 11:11 a.m. wasn't just the beginning of her fight; it was the awakening of mine. What came next wasn't a straight path to healing or success but a series of hard choices, relentless determination, and lessons forged in the fire of adversity. This is the story of how I crossed that bridge, one step at a time.

Four words, *24 hours to live*, would come to define my life after my daughter was born at just 25 weeks gestation, weighing only 1 lb. 11 oz. Those words weren't just a diagnosis; they were a constant refrain in my mind. There were countless days when doctors told me to prepare for her last moments, but I couldn't accept that outcome. My purpose became clear: to show up fully present every single day as the best version of myself.

Every morning, I arrived at the hospital on time, refusing to let the negativity surrounding her fragile condition seep into my mindset. I believed that if I wanted my daughter to have faith in her survival, I had to model that faith for her. My touch, my words, and my energy had to reflect unwavering hope. To do that, I had to operate with the highest emotional, mental, and physical performance possible. Showing up "whole" and "healed" became my daily mission, even as I faced exhaustion and fear. Fear, though silent, had been passed down like an heirloom, woven deeply into the fabric of my generational story. But here's the untold truth: fear doesn't decide who wins; *we do*.

Adversity is one of the greatest teachers. When my daughter and I were finally sent home from the NICU, it wasn't because she was fully recovered; it was because the doctors believed she would heal better outside the hospital. At home, life became a series of daily challenges. Machines kept her breathing, and I barely slept. But I realized that high performance isn't just about working harder; it's about aligning every action with purpose and efficiency. I had to learn to rest, care for myself, and build systems supporting her care and my own growth.

In this chapter, I'll share various lessons I've learned to overcome adversity, forge my purpose, and reveal the framework that helped me build resilience and elevate my performance. I turned vision boards into actionable blueprints, creating my M.A.P. (Making Action Plans) which is a person-centered planning method used to help individuals create a life plan by identifying their dreams, goals, challenges, and strengths. I realized that doing a good job wasn't enough; success required navigating the unspoken rules, understanding how to excel in new roles, and designing a path for success on my terms. Redefining my determination wasn't optional, it was essential. In the process, purpose became my anchor, grounding me in clarity, guiding me with intention, and propelling me toward peak performance.

From Breaking Point to Breakthrough

My corporate journey began in 2002, fueled by ambition but limited by inexperience in navigating complex organizational dynamics. From 2002 to 2014, I grew professionally through intuition and determination, but unresolved challenges persisted. By 2022, I was at a crossroads. Despite my professional success, I felt disconnected and overwhelmed, facing mounting workplace challenges and internal doubt. It was clear that continuing down the same path would no longer serve me.

A significant turning point came in 2022 when I began working with my therapist. This decision proved transformative as she helped me process workplace emotions and develop greater self-awareness. Through our weekly sessions, I learned to recognize patterns in my emotional responses and developed strategies to maintain composure during challenging situations.

In 2023, these skills were tested when an HR complaint emerged within my department. The feedback was personal and stung deeply. Initially, I felt anger and disappointment. However, therapy helped me step back, view the situation objectively, and recognize an opportunity for growth. I expanded my support system by engaging an executive coach who offered practical tools to transform challenges into opportunities. This combination of therapy and coaching became a pivotal moment in my leadership journey.

One resource my coach introduced was the book *The Coaching Habit,* which provided frameworks for fostering team collaboration and enhancing productivity. These principles aligned perfectly with my evolving leadership style, helping me strengthen alliances, improve team dynamics, and align organizational goals with purpose. This integration of emotional intelligence and strategic thinking marked the beginning of a profound transformation in how I approached leadership.

Faced with adversity, I made intentional choices. I worked hard to set aside my feelings of being attacked or the need to prove a point. Instead, I leaned into listening and leading with empathy. I reminded myself that two wrongs can exist at the same time and that people's actions are often shaped by their experiences, beliefs, and lived realities. This approach not only created psychological safety for my team but also for myself. I realized that the way we respond to adversity defines us as leaders. Leading with grace, even when it feels personal, but choosing empathy over ego has the power to transform difficult situations into opportunities for rising above with connection, growth, and integrity.

As I grew both professionally and personally, I realized that my purpose extended beyond survival or achievement. My goal was to thrive, at work, at home, and within my community. This required aligning every decision with a larger vision. Each action was filtered through the lens of purpose, ensuring interconnection between my work, relationships, and growth.

Leaning into my strengths became a key part of this alignment. I focused on solving problems, building systems, and driving results, all while refusing to let the chaos of my past dictate my professional identity. Clarity and focus became my most powerful tools, and I carried them into every project, every meeting, and every interaction. This alignment laid the groundwork for a broader evolution in my leadership approach, bridging purpose with a new set of tools for fostering emotional intelligence and strategic decision-making.

Through it all, I adopted a mantra that became my guiding principle: *Do hard things and do them well.* These six words reshaped the way I viewed challenges. They reminded me that true high performance isn't about achieving perfection, it's about resilience, self-awareness, and adaptability. It's about showing up, every single day, with the intention to excel, to grow, and to make an impact.

Purpose, however, isn't enough on its own. I learned that fulfilling a purpose requires intentional action, focus, and a refusal to succumb to mediocrity. I knew that to give my daughter the life she deserved, I needed to operate at my peak, mentally, emotionally, and physically. Each decision, no matter how small, had to be made with the long-term vision of building a better future. This mindset shifted how I approached life's inevitable hurdles. Difficult conversations and complex problems became opportunities for growth and refinement. I embraced challenges as pathways to learning and self-improvement. It wasn't always easy, but it was always worth it. The lessons I learned during this time became the foundation for a more intentional and impactful leadership style, setting the stage for deeper insights into emotional intelligence and strategy.

Lessons Learned in Emotional Intelligence and Strategic Leadership

I began implementing techniques that prioritized both emotional intelligence and business needs. During one-on-ones with my team, I focused on how they felt about challenges, providing them with a safe space to express concerns while emphasizing productivity and solution-oriented thinking. This dual focus helped my team avoid emotional stagnation and meet business goals.

At the same time, I learned to separate my work self from my home self. I worked hard during the day to meet organizational goals, but when I came home, I focused on my family. Therapy gave me the self-awareness to ensure I wasn't carrying the weight of work into my personal life. Mindfulness and meditation became daily practices, allowing me to process challenges without becoming overwhelmed. This balance was crucial for maintaining clarity and resilience in both spaces.

These lessons were especially critical in my high-stakes role of running a global program. When managing issues for hundreds of thousands of employees, I found that small problems could snowball into massive challenges if not addressed with intentionality. By prioritizing values, integrity, and flexibility, I learned to respond with curiosity and adaptability, ensuring my actions were both rational and measured.

It was during this time that I decided to chart my own course. While I continued to excel in my role, I began laying the groundwork for starting my own company. I realized I didn't want to be in environments that merely tolerated me. I wanted to create spaces that celebrated purpose-driven work and values-aligned leadership. Therapy and coaching gave me the confidence to take the same risks on myself that I had taken for the organizations I built stellar programs for.

Reflecting on my journey, I'm reminded of my daughter's early days in the NICU, moments when survival hung by a fragile thread. Watching her grow into a resilient and curious young woman, I realized those experiences shaped not only her life but mine. Surviving wasn't enough; I needed to thrive, for her and for myself. I wanted her to see, through my actions, that life's challenges could be met with purpose, strength, and grace.

Through this journey, I learned that challenges demand intentionality and adaptability. Life isn't about perfection, it's about showing up and committing to continuous improvement. With this clarity as my compass, I aligned my decisions with my values and professional goals, pursuing a life of fulfillment and impact.

In my career, clarity pushed me to embrace emotional intelligence and self-advocacy. I vividly recall the nerves of asking for pay raises when I realized I was underpaid, not for the money alone, but for equity. Advocating for stretch assignments, tackling tough projects, and presenting to senior leaders often left me feeling both empowered and emotionally drained. Yet, each act of courage strengthened my confidence and visibility.

Over time, I leaned into mentoring, fostering team connections, and seeking opportunities to lead at higher levels. I came to see self-advocacy not just as a right, but as a responsibility.

This evolution transformed how I viewed others. I began seeing my team as whole individuals, shaped by personal experiences, rather than just performance metrics. By fostering empathy and collaboration, I improved team dynamics and built trust. This mindset strengthened my leadership and taught me to navigate my own challenges with resilience and grace.

Building a Framework for Excellence: The Creation of P.E.A.K.

While navigating personal and professional challenges, I realized that both required more than sheer effort; they demanded intentional planning, self-awareness, and adaptability. From this understanding, I developed a framework that became my roadmap for operating at the highest level of performance. This framework, encapsulated in the acronym P.E.A.K., emerged through thoughtful reflection and deliberate action, particularly as I juggled the demands of a middle-management career and a busy personal life.

The school year was often the most challenging time. Between managing projects at work and supporting my family's needs, I found myself stretched thin. It was during these moments that I discovered the need for a structured, scalable approach to my goals. Vision boards and mapping exercises became my tools for clarity, helping me define and refine what success looked like for me. But tools alone weren't enough, I needed a framework that was grounded in both purpose and action.

The Elements of P.E.A.K.

Pragmatism: Balancing Vision with Actionable Steps

I learned that without pragmatism, a plan remains nothing more than an idea. It wasn't enough to dream big; I had to break those dreams into actionable, measurable steps. This meant balancing my professional ambitions with the realities of my personal life and ensuring both were aligned. Pragmatism required me to ask tough questions: *What's achievable today? What needs to wait? How can I make progress while remaining adaptable?* By creating a plan rooted in practicality, I was able to make steady, measurable progress in my career while finding fulfillment in my personal life.

Emotional Intelligence: Operating with Measured Emotions

My lived experiences and sensitivities shaped how I approached relationships, both at work and at home. I realized that my responses to challenges had a significant impact on the outcomes I achieved. Emotional intelligence became a cornerstone of my framework, teaching me to operate with measured emotions. I learned to recognize triggers, manage my reactions, and approach situations with empathy and thoughtfulness. This wasn't just about navigating interpersonal dynamics, it was about showing up as the leader, mom, friend, and mentor I aspired to be.

Acceleration: Taking Actionable Steps Toward Progress

A vision without movement is stagnant, and plans without action fail to deliver results. I recognized the importance of accelerating my plans by taking intentional, purposeful steps forward. Acceleration wasn't about rushing; it was about momentum. I focused on identifying opportunities to advance my goals, whether by taking on stretch assignments at work, refining processes at home, or investing in personal development. Each small action contributed to the larger picture, ensuring I was always moving closer to my goals.

Key Performance: Measuring Impact and Making Adjustments

I used to believe progress was all about effort, pushing harder, working longer, doing more. But over time, I learned that effort alone wasn't enough. Progress required measurement, clear markers to track impact and guide adjustments. It demanded honesty with myself about what was working and what needed to change, whether in my career milestones or in how I showed up for my family.

This realization didn't come easily. I remember the moments of doubt when I felt stuck, questioning if I was truly making an impact. Journaling became my anchor, a tool to document patterns and track what I now call Key Performance for Influence. It helped me see that success isn't just about external achievements but about alignment between my values, my actions, and the legacy I wanted to leave behind.

Through this process, I embraced and developed the P.E.A.K. Framework: Pragmatism, Emotional Intelligence, Acceleration, and Key Performance. It became my blueprint for navigating life's complexities with intention and grace.

I realized lofty goals needed to be grounded in practical steps and executed with clarity. "Balance" wasn't about splitting time evenly but about ensuring my actions were purposeful. In my career, this meant creating solutions that were realistic yet adaptable, making steady progress without losing sight of what mattered most, my family, my health, my purpose.

Learning to harness emotional intelligence was transformative. I stopped striving to be "right" and focused on being effective, controlling my responses, fostering collaboration, and creating an environment of trust. There were moments when my emotions got the best of me, times I felt overwhelmed by the weight of leadership or the fear of failure. But I discovered that emotional intelligence wasn't about suppressing those feelings; it was about channeling them to move forward with intention.

Acceleration became the catalyst that brought everything together. A plan without movement is just an idea, and I knew that progress wasn't always linear. It was about growing in knowledge, resilience, and emotional capacity, asking myself, *how can I grow as a leader, parent, or person?* Each step forward, no matter how small, created momentum.

One of the most profound shifts came when I began redefining success. It wasn't about climbing higher or achieving faster; it was about creating alignment and living my values authentically. I started tracking my progress through journaling, capturing the moments when I felt most in sync with my purpose. This intentional practice helped me transform setbacks into opportunities, redirect energy, and build influence where it mattered most.

The P.E.A.K. Framework became more than a professional tool, it was a personal philosophy. It guided me in mentoring young women, driving organizational change, and staying fully present for my daughter. It reminded me that progress isn't just upward; it's inward.

Operating at the highest level requires more than skills or strategies, it demands heart, adaptability, and an unwavering sense of purpose. By embracing these principles, I learned to transform challenges into stepping stones and leave every situation better than I found it. You can, too. With alignment, resilience, and intentionality, you can create a lasting impact in your career, in your relationships, and in your life.

Leveraging P.E.A.K. to Rise Above Adversity and Redefine Success

In the corporate world, I learned that being unseen and undervalued wasn't a reflection of my worth; it was an opportunity to redefine how I showed up. I began to advocate for myself, master strategic thinking, and navigate high-stakes environments with confidence. I learned that high performance requires boldness, vulnerability, and the willingness to embrace failure as a stepping-stone to success.

In my personal life, I applied the same principles. I realized that showing up for my daughter wasn't just about keeping her alive; it was about creating a legacy of love, stability, and opportunity. I wanted her to see, through my actions, that purpose and performance go hand in hand. It wasn't just about addressing the immediate challenges in my professional and personal life, it was about building a roadmap for sustainable growth and alignment. I recognized there were gaps in my professional development, and to close those gaps, I had to start with a foundation of intentionality.

Looking back, every hardship I faced was preparing me for a life of impact. From holding my daughter in the NICU to navigating corporate challenges, my journey has been defined by a relentless commitment to operating at the highest performance while staying deeply connected to my purpose. Purpose is the fire that fuels my drive, and performance is the vehicle that turns vision into reality.

Activity Section: Your P.E.A.K. Moment

Exercise: Think about a significant challenge you've faced. Write down:

1. The purpose that drove you to overcome it.
2. The actions you took to achieve your goal.
3. The lessons learned that could inform future decisions.

How can you use these insights to craft your own roadmap for high performance?

Conclusion

High performance isn't a privilege reserved for those untouched by hardship. It belongs to those who choose to align their actions with purpose, embrace failure as a teacher, and commit to continuous growth. My journey stands as proof that adversity doesn't define who you are, your response does.

For years, I carried the weight of an invisible clock, convinced I had just "24 hours to make a difference." This relentless urgency, compounded by my perfectionist tendencies, trapped me in a perpetual state of fight or flight. I was constantly racing to accomplish more, pushing myself harder, all while feeling like it was never enough.

My life and career changed immensely when I began to manage my time with intention. It was as though the chains of anxiety and urgency loosened their grip. I shifted from being a "super-doer" who prioritized tasks over impact to becoming a strategic visionary. I learned to focus not just on doing but on creating, not just on finishing but on transforming. This shift allowed me to step back, see the bigger picture, and steer my efforts toward meaningful, lasting change.

As my performance evolved, so did my perspective. I replaced the anxious drive to survive with a sense of curiosity about what I could achieve. I reframed my mindset, focusing on how to bring about optimal transformation both professionally and personally, balancing immediate goals with long-term vision. This was the true magic, marrying purpose with performance and infusing it with the pragmatism that made it all sustainable.

By letting go of urgency and embracing intention, I discovered the power of aligning purpose with action and how it could transform not just my work, but my life.

Adversity is not a barrier; it's a bridge. The question is, how will you cross it?

About the Author
Patrice Key

Global Social Impact Executive and Innovation Leader

Patrice is a dynamic and diversified social impact executive with over 22 years of leadership experience in IT software, telecommunications, and corporate sustainability. With an impressive track record at global giants such as AT&T and IBM, she is recognized for her ability to align innovative strategies with business objectives, driving measurable outcomes in highly competitive and rapidly evolving industries.

Her expertise bridges diverse organizational dynamics, spanning matrix, hierarchical, flat structures, and agency partnerships, across B2B, B2C, and B2G markets. Patrice has a specialized focus on AI, hybrid cloud, and telecommunications, enabling her to deliver transformative results that enhance brand value, attract investors, and strengthen competitive advantage. By anticipating trends and translating abstract challenges into actionable strategies, she has consistently driven innovation and impact across sectors.

Patrice's competencies include corporate governance, enterprise risk management, business process automation, and federal and state regulatory compliance. She is a pioneer in integrating social impact with technology, having reimagined IBM's $32M global workplace giving program into a scalable SaaS solution. Her work consolidated legacy tools, achieved a 26% growth in program engagement, and implemented operational sustainability strategies. At AT&T, she directed initiatives that resulted in a $20M corporate giving campaign while optimizing technology budgets to align with the company's strategic vision.

A dedicated advocate for corporate social responsibility, Patrice's leadership increased global volunteerism to over 900,000 hours and expanded diversity and inclusion initiatives, positioning organizations as trusted and purpose-driven brands. Her unique ability to align social impact programs with business goals help enhance reputation, build trust, and attract top talent in a multi-generational workforce.

Key Expertise:
- Corporate Governance and Policy Frameworks
- SaaS Implementation and Innovation
- Enterprise Risk Management and AI Integration
- Business Process Automation
- Federal and State Regulatory Compliance
- Corporate Social Responsibility and Communications

Patrice's visionary approach, strategic foresight, and commitment to aligning innovation with impact make her a transformative force in the fields of IT, telecommunications, and social responsibility. She continues to inspire organizations to create sustainable value, drive engagement, and lead with purpose.

Contact Information
Patrice Key
Website: https://socialvaluescollective.com/
Email: info@socialvaluescollective.com
Social: http://linkedin.com/in/patrice-key

IMAGE

AUTHENTIC PERSONAL BRAND, INFLUENCE, AND CREDIBILITY

Your leadership image is more than how you look; it's how you show up, make others feel, and command confidence in every room. Leadership effectiveness is not about being the loudest voice or the most extroverted person; it's about embodying credibility, authenticity, and the ability to inspire trust and respect. A strong leadership presence elevates not only your career but also the teams and organizations you lead.

True poise, power and presence requires the opposite of blending in, it's about owning your individuality, knowing the value you deliver, and having the courage to disrupt outdated norms. Whether you are rising as a young executive, or challenging conventional leadership norms, your personal brand should be an intentional reflection of your vision and influence.

When leaders project confidence, clarity, gravitas, and authenticity, they set the tone for their teams, create spaces of trust, and empower others to step into their own leadership identity. In the chapters ahead, our authors share how to cultivate an authentic and powerful image —one that commands attention, fuels career advancement, and ensures that your leadership is recognized, respected, and remembered.

Chapter 7

Becoming Chakla, Leading Boldly, Living Unapologetically

Embracing Purpose, Courage, and Authenticity to Inspire Others

Chakla Davis

Believing in the statement and not the question of "Why not you?" Absolutely unapologetically.

Introduction

My story is best described as a journey, a path shaped by courage, curiosity, and the determination to ask, "Why not me?" I am an African American woman from the rural South, with a US Southern accent, a unique name, and a small stature. From an early age, I thought differently and turned that mindset into a mission to inspire others to believe in their own potential: "Why not you?"

Hi, my name is Chakla Davis, and I want to share my journey of "Becoming Chakla" with you. Along the way, I've embraced four principles that guide me daily:

- Be vulnerable
- Trust in yourself
- Do the work
- Be unapologetically authentic

Overcoming Challenges: Turning Imposter Syndrome into Strength

I always did very well in school and knew it was the way to stand out at a young age. In junior high, I excelled academically and found myself in advanced math classes, often as the only African American and one of the very few girls in a room dominated by white males. This dynamic introduced me to imposter syndrome. Despite excelling, the weight of being the "only" made me question my place and often led me to conform to what others expected rather than showing up authentically as myself, as a child.

Yet, I used these challenges as motivation. I knew education was my way out of my small town and into a life of possibilities. As I progressed, I realized that succeeding in environments where I stood out required courage and curiosity. Over time, I reframed being the "only" into an advantage. My unique perspective became my superpower, allowing me to influence conversations and drive innovation.

Leading with Courage and Curiosity: The Disruptor's Mindset

Two words define my leadership style: **Disruptor** and **Authentic**. As a focus area of this chapter, I will guide you through pivotal stories with the intent of demonstrating how showing up with courage and curiosity does evolve into being a disruptive leader with authenticity and influence.

In the world of consumer product goods manufacturing (CPG) and other industries in Fortune 500 companies, I have often found myself as the "only", yet again, whether as the only woman, the only person of color, or the only Black woman in professional and leadership spaces. While this can be isolating, I have taken that circumstance, after many learning experiences and learned to leverage it as a superpower. Because I have a unique lived experience that gives me a different perspective, I now KNOW, it makes me very valuable.

I found my voice and have used it in a very unapologetic way, garnering a massive amount of credibility and respect as I lead in various forums and organizations. I tend to say the things that need to be said with the intent of progressing the conversation to a better outcome. I have led in both the private sector as well as non-profit Board service and leadership. As such, I am often sought after for thought leadership and being a transformational catalyst. It still feels strange to say the words "sought after," etc., but this is what WE have to be comfortable saying. When people give you your flowers, you have to accept them.

Early Leadership: Lessons in Vulnerability and Impact, not sure if this section fits

After college, I stepped directly into the world of Fortune 500 companies, working in manufacturing leadership. In these environments, power and influence were predominantly held by men. One man took me under his wing and gave me a piece of advice that has stayed with me: "How you start out is how you end up." These words carried significant weight, especially as a 22-year-old tasked with leading a team of individuals who were, on average, ten years older than me.

In that role, I learned to balance leadership with empathy. Initially, I tried to assert myself as "the boss," focusing on establishing authority rather than building understanding. It was a misstep born from insecurity and immaturity. My turning point came when I realized the importance of listening, not just hearing words, but understanding their meaning and meeting people where they were. Vulnerability became my greatest strength. When I stopped pretending to know everything and allowed myself to seek understanding, I earned respect and followership. This approach transformed my relationships and my ability to make an impact.

A Moment of Integrity: Finding & Trusting My Voice

Fast forward a few years to my role as an HR Leader for a manufacturing site in Georgia. Our site had a zero-tolerance safety policy, and one employee's violation led to an injury. According to policy, this violation required termination. However, the Site Leader hesitated, wanting to overlook the policy due to the injury.

I felt a deep ethical conflict. I stood my ground, telling the Site Leader that deviating from policy would undermine his credibility and erode trust in his leadership. I insisted that the executive leadership team weigh in if we were to make an exception. After deliberation, the decision was made to follow the policy. Later, both the Site Leader and the former employee expressed gratitude: the Site Leader for my courage and the former employee for my fairness.

This experience reinforced the importance of trusting myself and my values. Speaking up isn't easy, especially in high-stakes situations, but it's essential for authentic leadership.

A Defining Moment: Amplifying My Voice

One pivotal moment came during a relatively high stakes scenario in my first executive assignment as a Director of HR in a Fortune 500 company. During a talent review, we were discussing the succession plan for future Presidents of multi-billion-dollar businesses. The conversation was with the then Presidents of the businesses as well as my peers, and other HR leaders of those businesses; these were a subset of the top 10 leaders of the largest business in the entire company. Being new in my role, I felt the weight of the moment and it was a bit intimidating, even at my level. They were discussing profiles of future successors with what I felt was a very traditional lens. My hands were clammy, and I could feel my heart racing as I spoke up. I argued that we should consider skills like omnichannel expertise and innovation over just the conventional P&L ownership lens. To more clearly set the stage, each of the leaders in the room did not have this profile and did have the more traditional profile of progressive P&L ownership. My input shifted the conversation and reframed how leaders evaluated potential.

After the meeting, my leader pulled me aside and said, "This is your superpower. You added value and changed the trajectory of the conversation." That affirmation was pivotal. It confirmed the value of my voice and perspective. I realized that leaning into my expertise, being bold, and speaking up for what I believed in could lead to transformational outcomes. My leader at the time helped to reinforce the behavior, and that was the beginning of the "unlocking" of my voice and comfort level with using it and doing so unapologetically. She said, "You added value and changed the entire conversation to something more powerful. You think differently, and this is the role that I need you to play on the team." She said, "I need innovative and courageous leadership with new ideas, and this is the strength that you bring to the team."

Principles to Lead With Boldness and Purpose

My journey has shaped me into the leader I am today. My purpose is clear: to be bold enough to create opportunities for others who may not have had them otherwise. Throughout my experiences, four guiding principles have emerged as foundational truths that I carry forward:

- **Trust in Yourself**
- **Do the Work**
- **Be Vulnerable**
- **Be Unapologetically Authentic**

These principles are not just words; they represent the essence of my leadership philosophy and the lessons I've learned through my journey. Here is how each principle has played a pivotal role in my growth.

Trust in Yourself

As women, particularly women of color, we often find ourselves in spaces where our intuition and resilience are constantly tested. Our education, experiences, and the sheer determination that brought us here are powerful assets. Over time, I've learned that intuition, honed through life's challenges, is a powerful driver of decision-making, an art and science that requires calculated risk-taking. What I say to you is to lean into trust in yourself. You are here at this moment for a reason.

I vividly recall working as a site HR Leader in Arkansas when a colleague asked, "What do you want to do in your career?" My response was hesitant: "I'm not sure. I need to master this job." His reply was affirming and transformative: "You are the best HR Leader I've worked with because you lead with care and stand for what's best for people. You need to take on larger roles to broaden your impact."

That moment cemented my belief in my potential and sharpened my focus on leading with intentionality. Trusting myself became a daily practice, a reminder that I am in this moment for a reason.

Do The Work

Opportunities often come wrapped in challenges. They may feel daunting, exhausting, or even impossible. But every tough assignment is an opportunity to learn, grow, and stretch beyond what you think you're capable of. Doing the work with intentionality builds both intrinsic values, knowing you're capable, and external differentiation, shaping your brand and impact. You figure out what you like and have passion for, you get to learn from some and teach others, and you get to grow. Do the work with intentionality, and this will prepare you for your long-term potential as well as help you to define your own personal value proposition.

I embraced difficult assignments, from combining two businesses to leading HR for a $5 billion organization. There was a time when I worked as a regional HR Leader while managing a team on a different continent, starting my days at 3 a.m. to align with European work hours. Each experience taught me something invaluable about resilience, leadership, and my own capacity to excel under pressure.

Doing the work is about stepping out of your comfort zone and being intentional about your growth. It's about figuring out what fuels your passion, learning from others, and preparing yourself for future opportunities.

Be Vulnerable

Missed by many leaders, this principle is one of the most impactful. Leadership isn't just about metrics or goals; it's about people. The truth of the matter is that no matter what type of function or organization you lead, you are in the people business. If you hold to this core principle, most other things are simple. When you lead with empathy and openness, you build trust and inspire others to bring their full selves to the table. Your teams will be more open and transparent with you and will "run through walls" for you because they see your human side. In senior leadership, it is less about technical expertise and tactical execution; it is about asking the right questions to get to the best resolutions with empathy and vulnerability. Please remember, the more that your leadership roles progress, this is more and more important. When this happens, you are maximizing the experience of your people.

Be Unapologetically Authentic

Authenticity is a balance of skill and intention. It starts with trust, both in yourself and in those around you. Building trust requires open dialogue, humility, and a willingness to seek understanding. This trust building must be built on the assumption of positive intent. It also requires boldness: the courage to bring your voice to the table, even when it's uncomfortable. It means being bold in ideation, seeking first to understand, and providing feedback when necessary all with a lens of humility. The power of this skill is to not let the inner voices win that tell you to conform or hesitate to provide your opinion or input. When I started to bring my voice, my career trajectory took off as it was my differentiator.

I remember vividly a pivotal moment when a colleague acknowledged my ability to lead with care and connect the dots strategically. "You think differently," he said, "and that's what makes you stand out." His words empowered me to lean into my authenticity unapologetically.

Being authentic is about rejecting the urge to conform and instead using your unique perspective as a differentiator. When you embrace your authenticity, you lead with confidence and create a culture where others feel empowered to do the same.

Having Support is Essential

Having leaders who believed in me was critical to my growth. One leader's words still resonate: "I see your potential, and I'm investing in you." Their support showed up in tangible ways, stretch assignments, tough challenges, and opportunities that pushed me beyond my comfort zone. This was when I started seeing the potential and started assuming my whole purpose; being bold enough to be a servant leader without fitting in a box to please others and leading outside the box with the intent to bring others along.

Whether it was turning around engagement scores at a manufacturing site to achieve the highest in the consumer business globally or balancing complex roles across continents, these challenging experiences accelerated my growth. They taught me that confidence is built through action and that having a strong support system makes all the difference. These were all areas that translated to an acceleration of growth.... You are your greatest asset.

My Final Thoughts: You Are Your Greatest Asset

Currently, I am an executive HR Leader in a multi-billion-dollar organization where I influence at a broad level. I lead globally and regionally, with responsibility for several thousand people across various functions and expertise areas. I often think back to the engineering leader early in my career who told me, "You need to influence at a higher level because people need you." That wisdom became the foundation of everything I do and every decision I make.

Leading from the front means bringing my full self every day. It's about creating an environment where others feel empowered to do the same. Recently, two colleagues shared that they felt rejuvenated in their roles because of the authentic, human connection I bring to my leadership. One even offered to relocate to another country to support the vision I'm driving. These moments remind me of the profound responsibility we have as leaders, to show up, to connect, and to inspire.

As the year closed, my team gave me advice: "Take time for yourself and your family." One team member said, "This would be the greatest gift you could give us because we believe in your leadership, and we need you to show up as your authentic self. You can't do that if you're not recharged." Their words were powerful and humbling.

My purpose remains clear: to create opportunities for others who might not otherwise have them. I hope my journey inspires you to embrace yours. Let's lead with courage, authenticity, and the intent to make a difference.

Questions for Reflection:

- Are you listening to those inner voices that tell you to hold back or be smaller?
- Are you conforming to what you think is expected of you versus who you are meant to be?
- Are you creating an environment that cultivates trust and safety?
- Are you intentional in your journey to learn and apply your skills and capabilities?
- Are you being "you"?

Only you can answer these questions for yourself. My hope is that sharing my story has enriched your life and offered insight into the transformative moments that shaped me into the leader I am today. This chapter is meant to be felt, not just read, an experiential journey that highlights the importance of authenticity, courage, and purpose.

In the end, if we don't "each one, teach one," what are we doing this for? Let's create opportunities for those who might not have them and inspire the next generation of bold, authentic leaders.

About the Author

Chakla Davis

Innovative HR Strategist & Founder of

Bigby Davis Phoenix Rising Consulting

Chakla Davis was born and raised in Anderson, SC, and is a proud graduate of Clemson University, where she earned a Bachelor of Science in Management. She furthered her education with a Master of Science in Management from Southern Wesleyan University in Central, SC, building the foundation for a distinguished career in human resources and leadership.

With over 20 years of progressive leadership experience, Chakla has excelled in Fortune 200 companies such as Shaw Industries, a Berkshire Hathaway Company, and Kimberly-Clark Corporation, where she held multiple high-impact roles. Currently, she brings her expertise to Plexus Corporation in Neenah, WI, where she continues to shape innovative HR strategies and cultivate strategic business partnerships.

Chakla's career is marked by her creative approach to HR leadership and ability to drive transformation. Her extensive portfolio includes global and regional HR leadership roles across functions like Digital Innovation and Capabilities, Insights and Analytics, Brand Marketing, Supply Chain, Finance, and Research and Engineering. She also brings valuable experience in Manufacturing/Operations, Accounting/Finance, Mergers & Acquisitions, and nonprofit board leadership.

Recognized as a leader of influence, Chakla has earned numerous accolades, including being featured in *African-American Career World* magazine and named one of Wisconsin's *51 Most Influential Black Leaders* in 2023 by *Madison365*. In 2023, she served as Chair of the Fox Cities Chamber of Commerce Board, of which won the prestigious National Chamber of the Year award in 2024. Additionally, she is a McKinsey & Company Black Executive Leadership Program graduate, further solidifying her as a trailblazer in her field.

Chakla's commitment to making a difference extends beyond her career. She founded a scholarship fund, named the: Bigby-Davis Phoenix Rising Consulting, LLC Scholarship, to support students from her high school in

South Carolina, ensuring the next generation has opportunities to succeed.

Residing in Wisconsin with her husband, two children, and two dogs, Chakla embraces life to the fullest. A motorcycle license holder and adventure enthusiast, she embodies the philosophy that life is meant to be lived boldly and with purpose.

Contact Information:

Email: chakx2000@gmail.com
Facebook: https://www.facebook.com/share/1Aep2wDhS5/?mibextid=wwXIfr

LinkedIn: https://www.LinkedIn.com/in/chakla-davis-ms

Instagram: Instagram.com/chakladavis

Chapter 8

The Expert in the Room

Defining Leadership Beyond Age, Gender and Stereotypes

Que Parnell, PharmD

Have you ever felt invisible in a space, even though you were the expert, the leader?

Leadership as a young Black woman in corporate America is not just a role, it's a paradox. On the surface, it's a beacon of success, a hard-fought victory against the odds. But beneath the polished title lies a complex web of challenges, stereotypes, and silent battles. For many of us, stepping into the executive suite means navigating uncharted waters, where our presence disrupts traditional norms and expectations. Being both young and Black in leadership feels like walking into a room where the rules were written without us in mind, and yet, we're expected to excel without hesitation.

From a young age, I was taught that excellence was my ticket out, that defying the odds wasn't just a personal mission but a responsibility. But no one warned me of the emotional toll that would come with that pursuit. The quiet moments of being doubted, dismissed, or even invisible despite being the expert in the room. The unspoken reality that leadership at my age isn't just questioned, it's scrutinized. It's a dichotomy where achievement is celebrated on paper but challenged in practice.

Through years of self-reflection, I've uncovered a truth that many young female professionals of color experience but rarely articulate: the weight of breaking barriers is as heavy as the barriers themselves. Microaggressions, stereotypes, and societal expectations collide, leaving us to wrestle with questions that others never have to answer: Am I leading authentically, or am I overcompensating for a perception I did not create? How do I simultaneously pave the way and protect my own mental well-being?

Come with me on this journey, I'll take you inside a defining moment in my career, a high-stakes project with a multimillion-dollar budget where I faced invisibility head-on, even as the subject matter expert. You'll read about the pivotal encounter in a room full of decision-makers where my expertise was overlooked, and how one decisive moment shifted the entire narrative of leadership in that space. We'll explore the dynamics of asserting authority in environments where bias runs deep, and I'll share actionable strategies for navigating stereotypes and microaggressions to lead with confidence and impact. This is not just a story of survival but a blueprint for thriving in roles where you're underestimated.

For me, leadership isn't just about advancing my career, it's about dismantling the biases that tried to keep me out of the room in the first place. It's about proving, not to myself but to the world, that gender, youth, and Blackness are not hindrances but strengths. Still, I wonder: is the fight to redefine leadership and representation a triumph, or does it come at a cost too great to bear?

From Invisible to Indispensable: Reclaiming Authority in the Boardroom

The meeting was held in a sleek conference room on the 1st floor of our large corporate building. It was one of those rooms designed to intimidate, a long hardwood table surrounded by plush chairs, floor-to-ceiling windows offering a sweeping view of the massive parking lot, and the faint hum of fluorescent lights overhead. As I walked in, clutching my laptop and portfolio full of notes, I felt a mixture of pride and apprehension. This project, an extensive multimillion-dollar project handling medical specialty medications, was a career-defining opportunity, and I was the subject matter expert. Yet, as I took my seat near the center of the table, surrounded by older, predominantly Caucasian male colleagues and external vendors, the room seemed to shrink around me.

The energy was palpable, charged with a mix of anticipation and subtle power dynamics. As introductions began, I noticed the slight glances and the raised eyebrows as I stated my name and title. It wasn't overt, but I could feel it: the unspoken doubt. What is this little young Black girl doing here? As one of the few African Americans and even more noticeable women in the room, it was clear I was already an anomaly.

The meeting progressed, with each department presenting their updates. When it came time for the pharmacy segment, I straightened my posture, ready to command the room. But as the questions started, they weren't directed at me. One by one, the men around the table turned to my Vice President, an older white man seated in the chair next to me, and lobbed their inquiries his way, as though I wasn't even there.

I felt a flush of heat rise from my chest to my face, my palms slick with frustration. I had spent weeks preparing for this moment, delving into the data, refining strategies, coming up with questions and outlining solutions. And yet, it was as if my expertise was invisible, swallowed by the unspoken assumption that someone like me couldn't possibly hold the answers.

After I fired off a few questions, they attempted to answer and came back with questions of their own, but the questions and answers were not directed at me, they continued to address my counterpart. The struggle was real, knowing that I was the expert on the topic at hand, I sat back and watched the exchange. The Vice President, a seasoned professional with a no-nonsense demeanor, glanced at me question after question. He tried to answer to the best of his knowledge, but each time called my name to complete the thought and add more detail to the answers. Following the third question, I could see his patience wearing thin. Finally, he raised a hand to stop the flow of the conversation.

"She is the expert you need to be speaking to," he said, gesturing toward me. "Dr. Parnell leads this area and has all the answers you're looking for."

The room fell silent, the weight of his words hanging in the air. I watched as a flicker of surprise crossed several faces, some visibly taken aback. Slowly, the attention shifted to me.

In that moment, the energy of the room changed. I took a deep breath, steadying my voice and locking eyes with the attendees as I began to address their questions directly. The initial hesitation was palpable, but as I laid out the intricate details of the project, providing clear, concise answers, I saw a grudging respect begin to form. By the time I finished, the nods around the table weren't just polite, they were genuine acknowledgments of my expertise.

But beneath my outward composure was a whirlwind of emotions. Relief, yes, but also frustration. Why had it taken my VP's intervention for my voice to be heard? Why had my qualifications been doubted in the first place? As I drove the discussion forward, reclaiming my authority in the room, I realized this wasn't just a win for the project, it was a statement. A statement that leadership doesn't always look the way people expect, but it demands recognition, nonetheless.

By the end of the meeting, the questions came to me directly. The men who had initially bypassed me were now taking notes as I spoke, their earlier dismissiveness replaced by an attentive silence. I left the room with a newfound clarity: I had proven myself, but the fight for recognition in spaces like this was far from over.

Breaking the Mold: Redefining Expertise in the Face of Bias

The struggle for recognition is a quiet yet pervasive battle for young minority professionals, particularly those of us navigating fields long dominated by traditional leadership archetypes. Studies reveal that 67% of Black women in corporate America feel they must work harder than their colleagues to prove their value, and young professionals under 35 often report being viewed as inexperienced regardless of their qualifications. It's like showing up to a race with the fastest shoes, the best training, and a clear track ahead, only to find invisible hurdles placed in your lane, slowing you down before you even take your first step.

For many, expertise isn't enough. The room demands more: age, gender, appearance, and status symbols that align with outdated ideals of authority. It's a battle fought in boardrooms and on project teams, where contributions are often overshadowed by perceptions, and assumptions can cripple collaboration, stifle innovation, and drain morale. Research from the Center for Talent Innovation highlights that 41% of women of color feel "invisible" at work, an experience that is amplified in male-dominated industries. Imagine walking into a room wearing neon yet being treated as though you're cloaked in invisibility. It's not just frustrating; it's exhausting.

The weight was tangible for me during that meeting. As "the subject matter expert," I was not just prepared, I was ready to lead. Yet the constant redirection of questions to my

VP left me grappling with an inner conflict: do I assert myself and risk being seen as confrontational, or do I wait for recognition that may never come? It was an all-too-familiar dilemma for minority professionals, walking the tightrope between commanding authority and maintaining the delicate balance of workplace dynamics.

The defining moment came when my VP intervened, cutting through the layers of bias with a single sentence: "She is the expert you need to be speaking to." The room's collective response was almost audible, a brief pause, a flicker of surprise, and a perceptible shift in focus. It was like a spotlight finally turned toward the rightful performer on stage.

At that moment, I knew I couldn't let the opportunity pass. I leaned into my expertise, answering questions with clarity and redirecting the conversation toward the solutions I had meticulously prepared. With each response, I saw respect in the room grow, the earlier doubt melting away as my qualifications and confidence spoke louder than any title or demographic. It reminded me of the saying, *"When you know your worth, no one can make you feel worthless."* The challenge is ensuring others see that worth from the start.

This experience taught me a profound lesson: knowledge and skills are the ultimate qualifiers for leadership, but they must be paired with unwavering self-advocacy. While I was grateful for my VP's support, I reflected on what I could have done differently. Perhaps I should have asserted myself earlier, interrupting the pattern of redirection before it became ingrained. In hindsight, his intervention served as a blueprint, a reminder that sometimes, we need to demand the recognition we deserve, even if it means stepping outside of our comfort zone.

For young, minority professionals, these moments of acknowledgment are more than just personal victories. They're like cracks in a glass ceiling, small but pivotal signs that change is possible. Leadership can, and should, take many forms, and breaking the mold isn't a flaw; it's a necessity. But the question remains: how do we ensure that our voices are heard the first time, without waiting for someone else to validate them?

Turning Knowledge Into Authority: Strategies for Overcoming Bias and Asserting Expertise

The lessons I learned from that pivotal meeting weren't just about surviving a difficult moment, they became the foundation for how I lead, collaborate, and assert my expertise today. Overcoming bias and assumptions is never easy, but with intentional strategies, you can shift the narrative and take control of your professional presence. Here's how you can do the same.

Establish Your Presence Early: First impressions set the tone. From the moment you walk into a room, your demeanor, communication, and preparation should project confidence and authority. Think of it like laying a foundation: a strong start gives you a stable platform to build upon. For me, this meant arriving prepared with a clear understanding of my role, my value, and my goals for the meeting.

Know Your Brand and Value: Your professional brand is how others perceive your competence and character. Establishing your presence starts with knowing what you bring to the table and being prepared to articulate it. Before any meeting or presentation, I ask myself:

- What unique value do I offer in this space?
- What outcomes am I aiming to achieve?

By answering these questions, I position myself as a solution-oriented professional, which helps command attention early.

Practical Tip: Start meetings by confidently introducing yourself and stating your purpose. For example:

"Good morning, I'm Dr. Que Parnell, the pharmacy lead on this project. My focus today is to provide insights on the medical specialty drug strategy that supports this initiative."

This simple introduction signals your expertise and sets the expectation that your contributions will be essential to the conversation.

Use Allies Strategically: Even the most prepared professionals can face bias. In these moments, allies can help amplify your voice and reinforce your authority. My VP's intervention that day was a turning point, and it highlighted the importance of building relationships with supportive leaders and colleagues. Allies are individuals who recognize your expertise and are willing to advocate for you in challenging moments. Build these relationships by consistently delivering results, being collaborative, and showing respect for their expertise as well.

Practical Tip: If you know you're entering a potentially biased environment, brief an ally beforehand. For example:

"During the meeting, I'd appreciate it if you could help redirect questions about the pharmacy strategy my way so we can stay aligned."

This creates a subtle but powerful reinforcement of your role and ensures that others in the room hear your voice.

Redirect Conversations as Needed: When bias surfaces, redirecting conversations tactfully but firmly can reclaim your authority. During that pivotal meeting, once the VP directed questions to me, I had to ensure that the conversation stayed centered on my expertise. This involved confidently answering questions and, when necessary, redirecting follow-ups back to myself.

Take Control with Grace: When others inadvertently (or intentionally) overlook you, respond with clarity and composure. For instance, if someone redirects a question meant for you, say:

"Thank you for the question. I'd be happy to provide the specifics on that."

By calmly asserting yourself, you reinforce your expertise without creating tension.

Practical Tip: Use body language to emphasize your confidence. Sit upright, make eye contact with the person speaking, and lean in slightly when responding. These cues subtly convey authority and attentiveness.

Blueprint for Breaking Barriers: Steps to Stand Out and Lead with Authority

1. **Master Self-Advocacy Techniques**: Practice phrases that assert authority without sounding defensive. Examples include:
   - "I've researched this extensively, and here's what I recommend."
   - "As the project lead, I'd suggest we approach it this way."

Pair these statements with open, steady hand gestures and a calm tone to project confidence.

2. **Focus on Knowledge Mastery:** Expertise is the ultimate equalizer. The more you understand your subject matter, the more difficult it becomes for others to question your credibility. Dedicate time to continuous learning,

whether through certifications, industry publications, or hands-on experience.
3. **Leverage Visibility:** Use every opportunity to make your contributions known. Volunteer for high-profile projects, share your insights in team meetings, and seek opportunities to present your work. Visibility isn't just about being seen; it's about shaping perceptions of your expertise and leadership potential.

Owning the Room

As the meeting ended and I packed up my materials, I couldn't help but reflect on how close I had come to being completely overlooked in a room where I was the expert. The shift from invisibility to authority in that moment wasn't just a victory for me, it was a lesson in resilience, preparation, and the power of allies. But even more, it was a reminder that expertise isn't just about what you know; it's about how you claim the space to share it.

Throughout this chapter, we've explored the barriers young professionals, particularly minority women, face in traditional leadership spaces. We've delved into the stereotypes, the microaggressions, and the feeling of having to prove yourself tenfold just to stand on equal footing. Yet, the defining moment of recognition wasn't just a win, it was a call to action.

The truth is, that leadership doesn't wait for permission. It begins the moment you decide to own your expertise and use it to guide others. Your authority isn't tethered to how others perceive you; it's anchored in the confidence you have in your knowledge and the way you wield it.

But here's the question I leave with you: What will you do in your next defining moment? Will you wait for someone to redirect the room toward you, or will you claim your seat at the table with conviction?

As you reflect on these questions, remember this: true leadership transcends external biases. It's not about conforming to others' expectations but about owning your narrative and using your unique experiences to lead authentically.

Because the next time you step into a room, the question isn't whether you belong; the real question is how you'll use your presence to leave an indelible mark.

Owning My Legacy: How Visibility Became My Leadership Superpower

Today, I stand as an Executive Leadership Coach and Consultant, mentoring others and guiding organizations toward environments where everyone's expertise is valued and amplified. This journey from invisibility to authority has not only shaped my career but also deepened my commitment to creating spaces where others feel empowered to lead boldly.

That moment in the meeting room taught me a simple but profound truth: when you assert your knowledge, you change the narrative—not just for yourself but for everyone watching. And the confidence that comes from embracing your expertise has a ripple effect, opening doors you may not have even imagined.

About the Author

Que Parnell, PharmD

Transformational Pharmacist | Leadership Strategist | CEO of Monumental Enterprises

Dr. Que Parnell is a trailblazer who has redefined what it means to lead, inspire, and transform. As a Clinical Managed Care Pharmacist, Empowering Speaker, Executive Leadership Coach, and the visionary CEO and Founder of Monumental Enterprises, LLC, Dr. Que combines unparalleled expertise with an unwavering commitment to empowering others.

Her academic accomplishments are a testament to her dedication to excellence. Dr. Que holds a bachelor's degree in biology with double minors in chemistry and criminal justice, a Doctor of Pharmacy degree, and a master's in business administration. This robust foundation underpins her role as a thought leader in managing multi-million-dollar specialty medications for complex diseases, where she sets the standard for innovative care and strategic decision-making.

Dr. Que's impact extends far beyond the realm of pharmacy. She is the author of *Monumental M.O.D.E.*, a book and workbook designed to help individuals overcome unseen biases and self-imposed limitations. Through her podcast, *Monumental Mindset with Dr. Que,* she continues to inspire and motivate her audience to redefine success and pursue their greatest potential.

As the CEO of Monumental Enterprises, Dr. Que partners with Fortune 500 companies and forward-thinking businesses to provide leadership development and workplace culture solutions. Her work addresses critical challenges such as employee retention, cross-generational collaboration, and leadership readiness, delivering practical strategies that drive organizational growth and innovation.

Dr. Que's ultimate mission is to inspire individuals and organizations to unlock their full potential, achieve monumental goals, and build legacies that endure. Her empowering approach motivates clients to embrace their unique strengths and lead with purpose, ensuring they make a lasting mark in every space they occupy.

With her unique combination of technical expertise, strategic leadership, and an empowering mindset, Dr. Que Parnell is redefining what it means to lead and achieve at the highest level.

Contact Information:

Website: https://drquethecoach.com

Email: info@drquethecoach.com

Website: http://www.drquethecoach.com
Facebook: ttps://www.facebook.com/drquethecoach

Instagram: Instagram.com/drquethecoach

LinkedIn: dr-que-parnell-b175287a/

Chapter 9

Unapologetically Visible

Redefining Professional Image for Black Women

Shaunda Thompson

What if the key to redefining leadership isn't about fitting into a mold, but unapologetically shattering it with the full force of your authenticity?

On my first day as an adjunct professor, I stood outside the classroom door, my heart pounding louder than the noise of students filing into their seats. I glanced at my reflection in the glass window, adjusting the bright, patterned scarf wrapped around my natural curls, wondering if I was about to make a mistake by walking in looking like myself, vibrant, unapologetic, and very visibly me. I felt like an outsider in my own skin, and I worried that my presence, the bold colors, the statement jewelry, the natural hair, the unmistakable pride in my style, might seem out of place, a silent challenge to the stereotype of what a "professor" is supposed to look like. At that moment, I understood the weight of imposter syndrome that so many Black women carry in professional spaces, where the "norms" feel like they were designed without us in mind. But I also knew that to belong fully, I couldn't simply shrink to fit. I had to redefine the image of professionalism in a way that honored my identity and allowed me to lead with authenticity.

This chapter is an invitation to Black women to break free from the restrictive molds that tell us to conform and blend in, to silence our voices, and to tame our expressions. Through embracing personal style, natural hair, bold accessories, and vibrant clothing and rejecting these limiting ideas, I've learned that true leadership is about being unapologetically visible. Our power lies not in hiding but in standing out, in making room for our true selves in spaces that weren't always built with us in mind. For Black women, claiming this space means reshaping what our professional identity looks like and setting a new standard that reflects the richness of who we are. This chapter is a guide to transforming our professional image on our terms, stepping into each room with confidence, and inspiring others to see authenticity as a form of strength and presence that cannot and should not, be ignored.

Recognizing the Pressure to Conform

Stepping into professional spaces as a Black woman often feels like walking onto a stage where the script was written long before you arrived. The unspoken expectations press down heavily: keep your demeanor polished, your tones muted, your hair "manageable." Professionalism, as it's traditionally defined, seems to be a narrow box, one that ignores the richness and vibrancy of who we are. It's not just about appearance; it's about the subtle, daily pressures to tone down, to shrink, to mold ourselves into an image that feels foreign and restrictive. For years, I grappled with these expectations. Straight hair, conservative suits, a practiced quietness in meetings, it was a performance designed to fit a standard that wasn't created for me. I thought conformity was the price of admission to these spaces, the key to survival. But each compromise felt like a betrayal of my true self. Every time I silenced my voice or smoothed down my curls, I was telling myself, and the world, that my authenticity didn't belong. The cost was steep. I lost pieces of myself, little by little, until one day I looked in the mirror and barely recognized the woman staring back. These rules of "professionalism" were never neutral. They were built on a white, male patriarchy framework that excluded Black women, creating standards that felt suffocating and unattainable. The expectation to blend in, to straighten, to silence, to dim, was a reminder that these spaces weren't designed with us in mind. And yet, every time I compromised my authenticity to fit in, I moved further away from the ambitious and bold woman I knew myself to be.

These standards enforce conformity- Keep our wardrobe and style choices quiet, our hairstyles contained, and our personalities subdued. Natural hair? Too radical. A bold color? Too flashy. Confidence? Too intimidating. Self-expression has been weaponized to a set of rules that are foreign to us, and it takes an emotional tax on us. When we feel the need to dampen our light just to make others comfortable, the cost is steep. When I worked in the financial services industry, I remember vividly what it felt like to wake up each day and step into a version of myself that wasn't me. I would stand in front of the mirror, making sure no hair was out of place in my short, manicured pixie, buttoning up my conservative suits, and practicing a quieter tone. I was molding myself into the patriarchal image of a financial services professional, the image I thought would help me succeed. But every morning, as I transformed myself into this "professional" ideal, a little piece of me would slip away, and I could feel it. It was subtle, like a slow leak you don't notice at first, until you look around one day and realize how drained you've become.

As a Black woman in that world, I constantly felt the unspoken expectation to shrink myself to fit in. It wasn't just about how I looked; it was about everything: how I spoke, the words I chose, even how I held my body in meetings. I couldn't just walk in as myself; I had to monitor and adjust, like an actor rehearsing her lines, playing a role that felt unnatural. Every move, every word, every gesture was rehearsed and controlled, a measured attempt to seem "appropriate" and "professional." But underneath, I knew that none of it was for me; it was to fit the "standard."

I started to feel like an outsider in my own skin. Day by day, the small adjustments began to feel like betrayals. Each time I silenced my voice, smoothed down my curls, or dimmed my energy, I was telling myself that who I was wasn't enough, that my true self didn't belong in those rooms. And that quiet erosion of self, bit by bit, wore me down in ways I didn't even fully grasp until I was staring at my reflection, wondering who I had become. It's exhausting, heartbreaking even, to feel that you must constantly police yourself just to be accepted. And no matter how much I "fit in," it never felt like enough. I realized that the more I tried to meet these expectations, the further away I got from myself.

During my performance review, my supervisor leaned in and mentioned something unexpected. "I've noticed you often have a serious expression," he said, followed by, "and you're always taking notes in staff meetings." The way he said it, you'd think I'd done something wrong. I sat there, stunned, as he framed these habits, my focused attention and commitment to capturing every detail, as if they were shortcomings. It was jarring. At that moment, something shifted. I realized I was being judged not for my skills or my work ethic but for characteristics that reflected who I am, a Black woman in a professional space, serious about my work and unwilling to miss a beat. My diligence, my focus, and my intention to excel in that environment, these were seen not as strengths, but as somehow unfitting. It was as if my very presence, my professionalism in the way I naturally showed up, was being scrutinized for not fitting into some unspoken standard. That review was a wake-up call. I understood that no matter how dedicated I was, the lens through which my efforts were seen wasn't built for me. My seriousness and my note-taking weren't the problem. The problem was an environment that expected me to smile more, to soften myself, to perform a version of "professionalism" that felt hollow. That was the moment I decided I was done with shift-shaping to fit into someone else's mold.

I was done letting unspoken expectations chip away at my confidence. I decided right then to lean into who I am, to own my seriousness, my focus, and my dedication. If taking notes and wearing my focus visibly was a problem for others, that was not my problem to solve. I would no longer let anyone make me feel that my natural approach to excellence was a flaw. I realized I didn't need to adjust; what needed to change was the narrow, limiting view of what professionalism should look like. So, I took my first step: I started showing up fully as myself, without apology. In the next staff meeting, I wore my natural hair, in a tiny little afro, sat tall, took my notes, and made no effort to mask my focus or soften my presence. I asked direct questions, shared my insights with conviction, and didn't look around to gauge reactions. I was there to do my work, and I wasn't about to dim my light to make others comfortable.

That decision, that small but powerful action of simply being me, fully, boldly, and intentionally, was transformative. It marked the moment I reclaimed my confidence and owned my space, not as an act of defiance but as an act of authenticity. And from that day forward, I made a vow: I would never again let anyone else's unspoken expectations define how I showed up. This is my work, my voice, my presence. And that, exactly as it is, is more than enough.

Deconstructing Imposter Syndrome as a False Paradigm for Black Women

Imposter syndrome, for Black women, isn't a personal shortcoming; it's a mirror held up to a world that hasn't caught up to us yet. We're navigating spaces that weren't created with us in mind, so, naturally, it feels foreign. It's not about us not fitting in; it's about the spaces needing to broaden their definitions of who belongs. To truly address imposter syndrome, we must look at its source: the systemic biases, the narrow standards, the rules that favor one type of professional over others. The feeling that we don't belong isn't in our heads; it's in the very fabric of workplaces that lack diverse representation. This isn't about doubting our skills or abilities; it's about rejecting the biases that tell us we don't belong.

Belonging doesn't come from shrinking or from silencing yourself. True belonging is claiming your space with pride, knowing that your presence challenges and changes the environment. When you show up as your whole self, you redefine what it means to belong, and that transformation ripples out in ways that open doors for those who come after us. For me, that turning point came when I realized that my imposter feelings weren't mine to carry. They were the system's insecurities projected onto me. I remember sitting in a meeting, feeling like I didn't have the right to be at the table. But then it hit me: I had every right to be there. I didn't need to prove anything. My expertise, my experience, they speak for themselves. That was the moment I let go of those doubts and started to show up fully, knowing my place was earned and deserved.

The Turning Point; Owning the Room as Yourself

It takes a shift, a reclaiming of power, to go from self-doubt to self-assurance. Once I recognized that my authority was mine, I started showing up differently. It wasn't about seeking validation; it was about occupying the space I knew I deserved. Instead of walking into rooms trying to prove myself, I walked in claiming my space. This shift wasn't about arrogance; it was about affirming the years of experience and intelligence that brought me there. I prepared, not to convince others of my worth, but to stand firmly in it, to show up with the confidence that was always there. The question shifted from "Am I enough?" to the bold declaration, "I am more than enough."

Over time, I learned that people, students, colleagues, and clients don't want perfection; they want presence. People are not drawn to some polished performance but to authenticity, to someone who is real. For so long, I had felt the pressure to present myself in a certain way, to fit into the narrow mold of what a "professional" should look and sound like. I tried to be what I thought the job demanded: perfectly composed, detached, even a little distant. But over the years, I came to realize that those things were not my power; they were a mask hiding my true strength. In one of my early classes, I made a decision that changed everything. I put down the script, took off the mask, and chose to teach from a place of raw honesty. I let my voice and experiences guide the lesson, not some rigid agenda. I saw the shift immediately: my students leaned forward, eyes fixed, nodding along, hanging on to every word. They could sense that I wasn't performing; I was present. I was giving them the real me, not a sanitized version, and that was the energy that brought the room to life. I knew, in that moment, that this was how I was meant to lead.

True leadership isn't about fitting someone else's idea of what it should look like. I didn't need to be "polished," nor did I need to follow anyone else's rules. I needed to be fully present. When I owned the room as myself, I allowed others to show up fully, too. My students, my colleagues, my clients, they felt that energy, that honesty, and it gave them permission to be real as well. Authenticity is contagious. Showing up as my true self is what has made an impact, what resonates beyond any degree or title or polished façade. The world doesn't need us to conform; it needs us to bring the full force of our identities, our stories, and our experiences. And when I realized that, I knew I was done with performing. I was here to make a difference, not by shrinking, but by standing tall, by being exactly who I am. Now, when I walk into a room, I walk in as me. My natural hair, my vibrant voice, my unapologetic presence, I bring it all. And each time I do, I'm reminded of the power in that choice, of the impact that comes from showing up fully, deeply, and authentically. That's where my strength lies, and I will never go back.

Defining Style as Self-Expression

Style is more than clothes, colors, or fabrics draped over our shoulders; it's a declaration. For Black women, style is an act of self-expression that says, "I am here, unapologetically." We often step into spaces designed to contain us, to ask us to mold ourselves into someone's version of acceptable. But personal style, when embraced fully, becomes a powerful statement of authenticity, a way of introducing ourselves before we even speak a word. Our style tells the world, "This is who I am, and I stand proud in it."

For too long, the standard has been to tone it down, to dress "neutral" and blend in, to avoid anything too vibrant, too bold, too unmistakably us. But let me tell you, blending in has never changed a thing. In a world that still sees us as "other," our personal style is one of the few things entirely within our control, a piece of freedom we can shape to show up as our true selves. When I step into a room with confidence, charisma, natural hair and my bright, bold colors, I'm telling that room, "I belong here, just as I am." Style becomes a bridge, a way to bring our whole selves into spaces that might otherwise feel unwelcoming. Each choice, from a pair of earrings to a structured blazer in the most magnificent shade of turquoise, can be a tribute to our roots, our values, our individuality. That's the beauty of style as self-expression: it lets us take up space, boldly and beautifully.

The corporate world has long clung to a rigid idea of what "professional" looks like. But our presence challenges those outdated ideas, and our style can expand the definition of professionalism. Style isn't just about impressing or pleasing others; it's about shaping culture and influencing how people perceive strength and leadership. We're here to show that a bold, expressive style doesn't just fit within the frame of leadership, it enlarges it. When I began incorporating vibrant colors into my wardrobe, colors that spoke to my personality, I noticed a shift in how people responded. People would often say, "You bring so much energy into the room!" That's because color and texture speak a language of their own. A well-chosen accessory, a daring lip color, or a sharp, tailored suit in a deep jewel tone can make you memorable, leaving a lasting impression long after the meeting is over. When you express yourself boldly, you redefine what professionalism looks like, reminding others that leadership comes in many forms.

Let's debunk a few myths right now. Know that professionalism doesn't have to mean muted colors and fitted blazers devoid of character. It doesn't mean hiding who you are to make others comfortable. Bold patterns, statement jewelry, and natural hair aren't just appropriate, they're powerful. They're the foundation of authenticity and confidence, qualities every leader should embody.

Creating a Unique Professional Image

Creating a professional image as a Black woman means bringing your whole self into every space with intention, confidence, and pride. Our professional presence isn't just about appearance; it's a blend of how we look, carry ourselves, and communicate our truth. Here's how we can embrace each element to shine powerfully and unapologetically.

Our appearance is a statement of who we are. Style for us is more than clothing; it's identity, history, and self-respect. Choose pieces that reflect your power and make you feel grounded. Whether it's a structured blazer, a bold color that complements your skin, or a piece of jewelry that feels like home, let each item tell a story. Wear your natural hair, locs, or braids with pride, or go sleek and styled if that's your vibe. Let your appearance be your canvas, and don't be afraid to let it reflect all of you. How we carry ourselves often speaks before we even say a word. Show up with presence, grounded in the knowledge that you belong. Show respect, hold eye contact, and be fully present. Our warmth, our openness, our resilience, it's all part of the package. Engage with others with integrity, and when you speak, let it come from a place of power. Small gestures, like a warm smile or genuine acknowledgment, affirm your confidence and build respect. Our voices are powerful, and how we choose to use them sets us apart. Be intentional in what you say and how you say it. Speak with clarity and purpose, and don't be afraid to own the room with your perspective. When listening, lean in with empathy and respect. Whether it's in an email, a meeting, or a conversation, let your words reflect your strength, wisdom, and vision.

Impactful Moments with Style

Let me tell you about a moment when style made all the difference. I was attending an important industry conference, a room full of peers, thought leaders, and executives. I knew it would be a place to make connections, to leave a lasting impression. I chose an emerald green dress that felt regal, powerful, and grounded. I paired it with chunky, gold earrings that caught the light with every turn. My hair was styled in a crown of curls. As I walked through that room, people noticed. But it wasn't just the outfit, it was the confidence it brought out in me. I spoke with conviction, engaged with others openly, and felt an energy that came from embracing myself fully. By the end of that conference, people weren't just talking about my ideas, they remembered me. A woman even approached me later and said, "I admire how you light up the room and own your space. It's inspiring." That's the impact of personal style. It becomes a part of your identity, one that people remember, respect, and even aspire to emulate.

Style isn't a superficial detail. It's a medium, a message, a means of influence. Style is a way to rewrite the narrative, to say, "This is who I am, and this is what leadership looks like." We show that true leadership isn't about fitting into someone else's mold, it's about breaking it. How do we build a professional style that commands respect and feels true to who we are? Start with authenticity. Style isn't about following trends or fitting into someone else's box; it's about finding what resonates with you. Ask yourself, "What do I want my style to say about me?" Whether it's a soft but daring palette, a powerful silhouette, or a subtle nod to cultural heritage, your style should feel like a second skin. In practical terms, building a unique style is about knowing the staples that make you feel powerful and grounded. Identify your essentials: Is it a blazer that fits like a glove? Is it a pair of bold heels that lift both your stature and your spirit? For some, it's a color that makes their skin glow; for others, it's a fabric that moves with them. Once you know these pieces, build around them, layering in elements that reflect your personality, perhaps a statement necklace, a patterned scarf, or even a signature hairstyle. And remember, creating a unique image doesn't mean every outfit must be bold. It's about intentionality. Sometimes, a beautifully fitted neutral suit paired with an unforgettable accessory can be just as powerful as a colorful ensemble.

Style is about making thoughtful choices that let people see you, the real you, without compromise.

Embracing Natural Hair, Redefining Professionalism

There's a moment of undeniable freedom in letting my curls take center stage. Natural hair, for so many Black women, isn't simply a "style." It's a deliberate choice, a refusal to conform to standards that weren't built with us in mind. Wearing our hair in its natural state, coils, curls, locs, or kinks, is a way of showing up without apology. It's saying, "This is who I am, and this is professional, too." For me, embracing natural hair in the workplace was a turning point. It's more than a preference; it's a statement. In a world that tries to tell Black women to "tame" our hair, to straighten it, to make it "manageable," there's something powerful about saying, "No. My hair, as it grows, is perfect." My natural hair is part of my identity. It tells my story of resilience, of heritage, of authenticity. And when I walk into professional spaces, I'm carrying that history with me, proudly, unapologetically. Natural hair isn't just about how we look, it's about defying the unspoken rule that we must change ourselves to be accepted. And it's a reminder to ourselves, and to those around us, that our natural selves belong in every space.

Navigating Stereotypes

We know the stereotypes. Society has its labels for Black women with natural hair: unpolished, unprofessional, and even unruly. But these stereotypes have nothing to do with who we are; they're rooted in a history that wanted us to be anything but ourselves. And yet, for us, natural hair is a powerful statement of cultural pride, of authenticity, of resilience. It says, "I am here, and I will not change to make you comfortable."

Choosing to wear our hair in its natural state is often an act of courage. It means navigating the stares, the questions, and sometimes the silent judgment. But every day, more and more of us are choosing authenticity over assimilation. We're showing up as our full selves, and in doing so, we're redefining what it means to be professional. We're proving that natural hair and polished leadership are not only compatible, but they're also a force to be reckoned with. I remember the first time I wore my natural hair to a faculty meeting. I had just transitioned from straightening my hair daily, and it was still a new feeling, one I hadn't quite gotten used to. Walking in, I felt eyes on me, some curious, some confused. But I also felt a surge of confidence, a sense of pride. I was no longer hiding, no longer conforming. I was showing up fully as myself. At that moment, I felt like I was carving out space, not just for myself but for every woman who looks like me. It was a moment of quiet defiance, a way of claiming my rightful place in that room. And I knew then that I would never go back. That experience was empowering, a reminder of the strength that comes from being authentic. Style is more than fabric and color, it's how you tell the world who you are.

In spaces where conformity is the unspoken rule, a bold fashion choice can speak volumes. A pair of oversized earrings, a pop of color, or a statement dress, it's all a part of our self-expression. For me, wearing vibrant colors and bold accessories is my way of affirming my identity. Fashion becomes a personal shield, a way to walk into any space with the knowledge that I am my own person, that I am reclaiming a piece of the world for myself. In environments that weren't built with us in mind, every choice, our hairstyles, our colors, and our accessories become an act of resistance. By choosing styles that reflect who we are, we're reclaiming identity and setting new norms. We're showing that professionalism and authenticity can coexist.

Challenging Traditional Leadership Norms

When I wear my natural hair, my bright patterns, my bold accessories, I'm disrupting the traditional view of what a leader looks like. I'm challenging the narrow definitions of professionalism, expanding the narrative of what authority and expertise can look like. I want people to see that leadership isn't about fitting into a box; it's about creating space for others to show up as they are, too. I'll never forget the day a student, a young, black woman who aspired to be a Neuroscientist, approached me after class. She said, "Seeing you with your natural hair and bold earrings makes me feel like I can do the same. I don't have to hide." That moment was powerful because it reminded me that our choices, our authenticity, can inspire others. By showing up as ourselves, we give others permission to do the same. We create a ripple effect of confidence, authenticity, and pride.

For Black women, leadership is about creating spaces where we can be fully seen and heard, where our whole selves are celebrated and embraced. The traditional image of leadership is often steeped in conformity, but we're here to change that. We're here to show that leadership isn't about checking boxes or fitting in. It's about creating spaces where difference is valued, where authenticity is the rule, not the exception. By embracing leadership on our own terms, we open doors not just for ourselves but for those who come after us. Authenticity builds trust. When we show up as ourselves, we connect with others in deeper, more meaningful ways. Students, colleagues, clients, they respond to realness. They see themselves in us, see the possibility of being their true selves, too. Authenticity isn't just an asset; it's a superpower that lets us lead with empathy, strength, and impact.

Black women in leadership aren't just stepping into roles; we're transforming them. We're showing that professionalism doesn't have to look one way, that expertise isn't tied to a single aesthetic. By embracing our full selves, we expand what leadership looks like, creating a more inclusive, dynamic model that celebrates diversity. Every day, Black women in professional spaces are redefining what it means to lead, to be authentic, to take up space.

Whether it's through natural hair, bold fashion, or unwavering authenticity, we're creating a new narrative.

We're showing that true leadership doesn't come from conforming; it comes from embracing our power, our culture, our unique voices. And in doing so, we're opening doors, setting new standards, and inspiring others to step into their full selves. Our presence, our authenticity, and our style are a testament to resilience, to beauty, to strength. This is what it means to lead on our own terms. Looking back on my journey, I see a path carved out of courage and a fierce commitment to overcome imposter syndrome. Like many Black women, I once felt the weight of needing to fit a standard that wasn't built with me in mind. But the more I tried to blend in, the more I realized that true leadership doesn't come from hiding who we are, it comes from embracing it fully.

Navigating this journey requires intentionality and a commitment to both authenticity and strategy. Small, deliberate steps can help build confidence and ensure that showing up boldly enhances, rather than hinders, career progress. Here are some actions that women, particularly Black women, can take to challenge traditional norms while thriving professionally:

Start With Self-Acceptance

Embrace who you are and recognize that your authenticity is your power. Spend time identifying what makes you unique and reflecting on how those traits contribute to your strengths as a leader. This self-awareness is foundational for showing up unapologetically.

Redefine Professionalism for Yourself

Begin by questioning the traditional standards of professionalism and how they align (or don't align) with your values. Identify the aspects of yourself you want to bring into the workplace and make deliberate choices that reflect your authenticity, whether that's through your fashion, your hair, or your voice in meetings. Own your space and make it clear that professionalism can and should encompass diversity.

Set Boundaries Around Your Authenticity

While being authentic is powerful, it's also important to protect yourself in environments that might not be immediately welcoming. Set clear boundaries for how much of yourself you choose to share and in which spaces. For example, you might start with subtle changes like incorporating small personal touches into your attire or speaking up in areas where you have expertise.

Master Your Craft

Authenticity and excellence go hand in hand. By consistently delivering high-quality work, you not only build credibility but also demonstrate that authenticity doesn't detract from professionalism, it enhances it. Let your performance speak for itself while your presence challenges stereotypes.

Normalize Your Presence

Each time you show up authentically, you chip away at the narrow definitions of leadership. Consistency is key. When others see you owning your space unapologetically over time, it challenges their biases and helps normalize diversity in leadership.

Communicate With Confidence

Boldness doesn't have to mean being confrontational. Practice speaking up with clarity and conviction, ensuring your ideas are heard and respected. Be intentional about using "I" statements and avoid over-apologizing or diminishing your contributions.

Celebrate Small Wins

Every time you wear your natural hair to a big meeting, express your unique perspective in a group setting, or receive positive feedback for your authenticity, take a moment to celebrate. These small victories reinforce your confidence and remind you of the impact of showing up fully as yourself.

Educate Others Along the Way

Sometimes, the resistance to authenticity stems from a lack of understanding. Where appropriate, use your presence as an opportunity to educate and build awareness about the value of diversity in leadership. Share your experiences, but only when you feel safe and empowered to do so.

Showing Up Boldly Without Negatively Affecting Your Career

Own Your Narrative: Reclaim the story of who you are and why your authenticity matters. Frame your presence as a leadership asset rather than a deviation from the norm.

Focus on Your Allies: Build relationships with colleagues, managers, or organizational leaders who champion inclusivity and can amplify your voice.

Leverage Emotional Intelligence: Navigating bias and resistance requires a mix of awareness, strategy, and emotional control. Start by recognizing your own emotions in the moment, are you feeling anger, frustration, or hurt? Taking a deep breath and centering yourself can help you respond from a place of clarity rather than reacting impulsively. Approach the situation with tact by addressing the behavior or comment. For example, instead of saying, "You're being biased," you might say, "I noticed that this perspective wasn't included, can we explore it further?" This keeps the focus on the issue, not the person, and encourages collaboration. Empathy is another powerful tool. Try to understand where the other person is coming from, even if their perspective is rooted in bias. This doesn't mean excusing harmful behavior but rather acknowledging that change often comes through dialogue and understanding. For example, if someone makes a comment rooted in a stereotype, you might respond with, "I hear what you're saying. Let me share another perspective based on my experience." This approach can defuse defensiveness and open the door for learning. At the same time, set clear boundaries. Emotional intelligence doesn't mean tolerating disrespect or diminishing your voice. If a situation calls for it, assert yourself calmly but firmly. For instance, you might say, "I value open dialogue, but it's important that all voices are heard and respected in this space." By balancing tact, empathy, and self-assuredness, you can challenge bias effectively while maintaining your authenticity and protecting your peace. This not only preserves your credibility but also sets a standard for how you expect to be treated.

Know When to Push and When to Pause: Pick your battles wisely. Not every situation requires a bold stand, sometimes subtlety and patience yield better results.

In Closing

Authenticity is not a one-time decision; it's a daily commitment to stand in our truth and redefine what leadership looks like on our terms. Leadership that embraces individuality is leadership that inspires change and opens doors for others. For every Black woman who's felt the tension between staying true to herself and meeting societal expectations, let this be your reminder: standing out is your superpower. Here are three powerful steps to start your journey toward unapologetic authenticity:

Show Up Fully, One Step at a Time. Choose one aspect of yourself, your natural hair, a vibrant color, or a bold accessory, and wear it proudly in spaces where you may have once held back. This isn't just about fashion; it's a declaration that you're here to be seen, heard, and respected for who you truly are.

Speak Your Truth Boldly. Step into conversations, meetings, and discussions with the courage to share your unique perspective. Your voice carries power and perspective that can change the conversation, inspire others, and elevate the room.

Build a Circle of Authentic Empowerment. Surround yourself with other women who champion authenticity. Create a network that lifts you up, celebrates your successes, and stands beside you in moments of challenge. Each of these actions is a step toward embodying a leadership style that's genuine, bold, and impactful. As you embrace your authentic self, you set a powerful example for others, showing that leadership is strongest when we bring all of who we are. Take up space, walk with pride, and let the world see the powerful, unapologetic leader you are.

About the Author

Shaunda Thompson

Career Strategist | Certified Career Coach | Image Consultant | CEO

Shaunda Thompson is a dynamic force in career development, blending two decades of expertise with an unwavering passion for empowering individuals to achieve professional and personal excellence. Shaunda has transformed the trajectories of countless professionals across government, nonprofit, and educational sectors as a Career Strategist, Certified Federal Career Coach, Certified Interview Coach, and Certified Federal Job Search Trainer.

Her journey as a mentor and leader began during her distinguished military service as a Non-Commissioned Officer in the United States Army. There, she honed her skills as a motivator and mentor, inspiring subordinates and peers to unlock their potential and achieve greatness. This foundational experience ignited her passion for coaching, which has since blossomed into a career defined by transformational impact.

As a 2x Best-Selling Author, Image Consultant, and the CEO of her own career consultancy, Shaunda helps clients redefine their professional identity, build a powerful personal brand, and elevate their presence. Her holistic coaching approach, infused with her signature candor, combines personality development with image enhancement to guide clients toward reclaiming their confidence and embracing their full potential.

Shaunda's credentials include certifications in CliftonStrengths, MBTI, and What's My Communication Style assessments, enabling her to tailor strategies that align with her clients' unique needs. Known affectionately as Coach "T," she has delivered impactful leadership development training for esteemed organizations such as the U.S. Department of State's International Visitor Leadership Program, Orange County Public Library, and the Society for Human Resource Management in Atlanta.

At the heart of Shaunda's mission is a profound belief in helping individuals shine unapologetically in their careers and lives. She inspires transformation, turning ambitious visions into actionable realities while equipping clients with the confidence, clarity, and purpose they need to thrive.

Shaunda Thompson's proven expertise, infectious enthusiasm, and ability to unlock untapped potential make her an indispensable ally for anyone seeking to elevate their career, amplify their brand, and achieve unparalleled success.

Contact Information:

Shaunda Thompson
Web: www.shaundathompson.com
Email: Contact@shaundathompson.com
Social: IG- @shaundawrites

COMMMUNICATION

The Art of Influence and Advocacy

Your ability to articulate ideas, advocate for yourself and others, and command attention in the right rooms is what sets you apart as a leader. The most successful leaders do not just share information; they inspire action, navigate difficult conversations with confidence, and use their voices to create lasting impact.

Communication is a strategic tool, not just a skill. Whether you are persuading stakeholders, advocating for your ideas, or leading through change, your communication determines how your leadership is perceived and how far your influence extends. Redefining leadership means shifting from simply being knowledgeable to being influential, ensuring that your voice shapes decisions, drives progress, and challenges outdated leadership norms. The leaders of the future will not be defined by their titles alone but by their ability to articulate a vision, align people around a common goal, and foster dialogue that leads to transformation. In the chapters ahead, our authors explore the power of executive communication, the nuances of influence, and the importance of speaking with intention, ensuring that your voice becomes one of your greatest leadership assets.

Chapter 10

Authentic Advocacy in Action

Owning Your Voice and Vision

Juwayriyah Hussain

"Self-promotion is a delicate dance between showcasing your strengths and not coming across as boastful." –
Unknown

No one wants to come across as a braggart, sleazy, arrogant, or the worst 'that person.' As women, we're particularly more sensitive to it. We have to walk the tight rope, because backlash and punishment for us is severe. According to a 2022 study, women are 24-31% less likely to self-promote than their male counterparts. The most common reasons include fear of backlash, negative bias, discomfort with self-promotion, and a perception that it lacks authenticity. These challenges often lead to hesitation, causing many women to miss out on opportunities to showcase their value and advance their careers.

Yet, the contradiction is clear: leadership, whether by authority or influence, requires a strong ability to self-advocate and communicate your value. This paradox creates an emotional and professional dilemma for many women, demoralizing us from attempting self-promotion altogether. As women, we are conditioned to be meek, humble, and self-effacing, often taught from a young age that these qualities are virtues. Society reinforces this expectation in professional spaces, penalizing assertiveness or confidence that deviates from traditional norms. The result is a lack of visibility, stalled career progression, and missed leadership opportunities.

But it doesn't have to be this way. There *is* a way to break through this paradox, and it starts with redefining communication and leveraging the natural strengths many women already possess. By reframing self-promotion as authentic storytelling, we can tap into women's superior communication skills to elevate our professional presence and open doors to leadership.

Throughout my career, I've witnessed firsthand how these challenges play out. Early in my journey, I believed communication was about presenting ideas, delivering emails, or perfecting the occasional meeting or presentation. Professional training taught me to focus on word choice, tone, and body language, all while avoiding repetition unless it added value. These lessons served me well for day-to-day work, but they left me woefully unprepared for advocating for myself.

When I began promoting my accomplishments, I felt uncomfortable, inauthentic, and full of self-doubt. My tongue grew thick as I forced out what felt like bragging, but I thought I could get used to it. With no alternative approach in sight, I pushed forward, trying to mirror my (all-male) peers. Six months later, I hit a massive brick wall, realizing that not only was my approach unsustainable, but it also wasn't effective.

In this chapter, I will share the lessons I've learned, the strategies I've refined, and the insights I've gained about the power of effective communication, self-advocacy, and personal branding. Together, we'll explore how women can overcome societal conditioning, break through professional barriers, and advocate for themselves authentically without selling out. By understanding why self-promotion is so difficult and learning how to approach it differently, you'll be equipped to take control of your narrative and lead with confidence. Let's get started.

Is Perception Reality?

I sat alone in the conference room staring blankly at the results from my 360 evaluation. "Top performer," "Aggressive," "Intimidating." Are you F%$*ing kidding me!? The words screamed at me from the page. I was shaking with rage in that cold, outdated 80's era conference room with the large oak table, engulfed by one of those giant black plastic "leather" executive chairs meant for a 6 foot tall man. I sat rereading the words over and over again, looking for something different. These words were foreign. This feedback from my carefully selected list of peers, managers and directors made no sense, well to me at least.

Top performer, yes, absolutely! I've had excellent performance reviews for the last four years and have been promoted twice, faster than anyone else on the team. I was the "go to" person for not only my boss, but my director as well. But aggressive? Intimidating? How could anyone consider my petite little 5-foot tall, introverted self that shared homemade cookies and smiled at everyone in the hallways intimidating?! I was glad I was alone. I walked out of the conference room in a rage, eyes brimming with angry tears. Thank goodness it was late on a Friday afternoon and the office was nearly empty. I packed my things and hoped I wouldn't run into anyone on the way to my car. The day I received my 360-evaluation feedback changed everything for me.

Where I thought I had been clear, assertive and confident, I was perceived as "aggressive" and "pushy". To put it mildly, I was frustrated and confused. I couldn't understand why I didn't receive the same recognition and opportunities after killing it across multiple projects and presentations. It wasn't until I realized that for women, the rules were different. It's insufficient to do the work and promote your accomplishments.

Three Lessons from a Hard Truth

That 360-evaluation experience changed my entire perspective on how I needed to promote myself. I thought about it all weekend and by Monday morning had learned three things:

1. **Feedback is a gift, but you don't have to accept it.** Not every piece of feedback is valid or actionable. It's important to separate constructive criticism from biased perceptions.
2. **Perception *is* reality.** If people see me as aggressive or intimidating, their perception becomes my professional reality. I needed to acknowledge this and find a way to reshape it.
3. **I need a different strategy.** I couldn't rely on the same self-promotion tactics my male peers used. I

needed an approach that worked for me, authentic, intentional, and grounded in who I am.

The Challenge to Market Myself

Feeling proud of my growth and insights, I scheduled a meeting with my mentor that Monday afternoon. As I shared what I'd learned, he nodded and acknowledged my hard work. Then, he said something that stuck with me:

"This is all good work. Now you have to *market yourself*." The real you.

I nodded in agreement, thinking I understood. But it wasn't until later, when I began working in marketing, that I truly grasped the meaning of those words. Marketing yourself isn't about bragging or inflating your accomplishments. It's about creating an authentic narrative that highlights your value in a way others can't ignore.

In the next section, I'll explain what it really means to market yourself effectively and authentically without losing your integrity or compromising your values.

Here's an analogy that is marketing-based since that's my world. Think of content as the message, the story, or the product, like a video you create. The activation is the mechanism or vehicle you use to share that content with the world, like posting the video on YouTube, emailing it to friends, or sharing it on social media platforms. The success of content depends heavily on the activation vehicle or mechanism used. A brilliant video that isn't shared widely will only reach a handful of viewers, while the same video, strategically activated with keywords and tags, using multiple platforms, has the potential to go viral.

This realization became a significant turning point in my professional development. My performance, many accomplishments, and personality were my content. I communicated my work and impact through the activation, the vehicle to ensure my contributions were seen, valued, and understood. I had to choose the right vehicle, specifically designed for me.

Reframing Feedback: The Strategic Pivot

When I revisited the feedback from my 360 evaluations, I had a choice to make. Should I accept being perceived as "aggressive" and "intimidating," or could I reshape my narrative into something more aligned with my goals? I decided I wanted to embrace "aggressive" as ambitious and I had to choose how to position it to my advantage, but "intimidating" didn't serve me.

To shift perceptions, I needed to change my approach. I reflected on the marketing lesson about content and activation. While my content, my performance, was solid, my activation, the way I communicated, the vehicle I chose needed adjustment. I needed to find a formula for my activation, instead of using someone else's formula. I resolved to close the gap between how I was currently perceived and the personal brand that would be authentic to me: *aggressive yet collaborative, capable yet kind. That felt aligned.*

Trial and Error: My Path to Intentional Branding

I didn't have a manual, guide, blueprint or successful female role model to learn from, so like everyone else, I started with trial and error. I started small, in my one-on-ones with my manager, I would share my accomplishments for the month and pay close attention to what captured his interest. I knew complaining about work was a favorite pastime, so I employed what we now call "humble bragging." Statements such as, "I keep getting bigger projects," "I have so much work," "Anything my boss needs he comes to me first," "I had to redo everything I got from the other team," etc. Sometimes it landed well, other times it bombed, but eventually, I started to see what was working and got more comfortable. The point is, once I became intentional that I wanted to be perceived as exacting, and approachable, I consistently framed my accomplishments to reinforce that, eventually making it my reputation. I became a highly desired mentor and was quickly promoted to manager.

I committed to framing my accomplishments in ways that reinforced the qualities I wanted to be known for. If I wanted to be seen as collaborative, I emphasized teamwork in my successes. If I wanted to highlight my approachability,

I shared stories that showcased my kindness or empathy in challenging situations. Slowly but surely, the gap between my current reputation and my desired personal brand began to close. This wasn't just about getting a title; it was about aligning my actions, communication, and values to create a reputation that truly represented me.

The Turning Point: The Strategic Pivot

Being intentional about communicating my strengths and accomplishments helped shift my brand to where I wanted it, but I still wasn't seeing the career progression I desired. Specifically, I wasn't getting promotions. Twice, I was passed up for candidates with similar experience but far fewer accomplishments. Frustration set in after a third promotion went to the guy four cubicles over. Determined to understand why, I scheduled a feedback session with the hiring manager, my director.

I spent the two weeks leading up to the meeting nervous and anxious. Every day, I would swing like a pendulum between keeping or cancelling the meeting. Eventually the day came, and I couldn't focus. I sat staring blankly at my computer, watching minutes turn to hours. When the calendar reminder told me I had 15 minutes, my throat went dry, the speech I had been drafting for two weeks jumbled in my head and every muscle in my shoulders tensed, curled inwards, willing me to turn into a ball and roll away. Eventually, I stood, shook my shoulders out, took two deep breaths and walked into the director's office.

I shut the door, sat down and without any small talk, asked the only question that mattered in my mind, "Why didn't I get the job?"

His answer? "We don't know what you want."

His response left me speechless. Obviously, the promotion, DUH! I thought! But what I said was "I'm not following, can you explain what you mean?"

In paraphrasing words, I didn't get the promotion because the leadership on the interview panel didn't believe I had clear career goals and aspirations, so they weren't sure this promotion would be a good long term fit for me. In layman's terms, they didn't know what my end game was.

I walked out of his office stunned and still a bit confused. I heard their reasoning, but I didn't fully understand it. I had worked so hard to establish my brand, communicate my accomplishments, and be a top performer. I knew the leaders saw my value; it was in my interview feedback. But at that moment, I realized I had neglected one critical piece of the puzzle: articulating my purpose, desired outcomes, and career strategy.

This feedback became a turning point for me, a moment of clarity that changed the way I approached my career. As I previously mentioned, I didn't have a roadmap or mentor; this was trial and error, and I realized the error. It wasn't enough to simply jump in and do the work, promote my accomplishments, or even shift perceptions. The flaw: I started with tactical actions; I needed a purpose-driven personal brand and strategy that others could see and support. Leaders needed to understand not only what I brought to the table but also where I wanted to go and how I intended to get there. Sharing my desired outcomes, career aspirations, and impact strategy with key stakeholders became the missing link that aligned my goals with opportunities.

This pivotal realization taught me that self-advocacy isn't just about marketing yourself; it's about creating a clear career roadmap and inviting others to join you on the journey. It's about showing and articulating your vision and making space for others to help you achieve it.

The Art and Science of Creating an Authentic Brand You Can Articulate

Building a strong personal brand requires intentionality, strategy, and authenticity. For women, the challenge often lies in balancing the desire to showcase their achievements with the fear of being perceived as boastful. However, cultivating a personal brand is not about seeking attention, it's about creating a clear, compelling narrative of who you are, what you stand for, the value you bring and what you aim to achieve. Personal branding, paired with effective communication, can shape how you're perceived, establish credibility, and unlock career opportunities.

In this section, I'll share four key strategies that transformed how I communicate and activate my personal brand. These strategies, getting clear on desired outcomes, seeking feedback, embracing authenticity, and making communication a consistent habit, are powerful tools to align perception with purpose and amplify your impact.

4. Get Clear On Your Desired Outcome

Understanding your desired outcome is the foundation of effective communication. Every interaction should serve a purpose, whether an email, presentation, or conversation. Your message becomes focused, targeted, and impactful when you're clear on what you want to achieve.

Early in my career, I often defaulted to vague outcomes like "share information" or "make a decision." With coaching and practice, I shifted to specific goals like "secure explicit commitment for resources" or "align on priorities to meet a deadline." This clarity transformed my communication, making my requests compelling and actionable.

A tool I regularly rely on, based on the Socratic Method, is what I call the "5 Why's" method, which refines the purpose behind your communication:

1. Start with your basic desired outcome and write it down.
2. Ask, "Why is this important?" Write the answer.

3. Repeat the "why" question four more times, refining your purpose with each step.

Here's an example from a midyear review presentation to executive staff:

- **Initial outcome:** Share year-to-date budget spend.
- **Why?:** To help management understand the burn rate.
- **Why?:** To show our forecast projects a budget overrun.
- **Why?:** To justify an additional $100K budget request.
- **Why?:** To avoid putting goals at risk.
- **Final Why?:** To secure a decision on adjusting goals or allocating more budget.

In this example, if my desired outcome had been to inform the staff of the current budget, that presentation would have been extremely different, and frankly underwhelming in comparison to the REAL desired outcome of having a directional decision on spend vs goals. Being critical of your desired outcome to push for a more meaningful outcome will completely change how you communicate. By focusing on the deeper purpose, I reframed my presentation to tell a story, build a compelling case, and achieve a meaningful result.

Similarly, defining your desired outcomes for personal branding ensures your efforts are intentional and aligned with your goals. With repeated practice, having a clear desired outcome becomes a very powerful communication habit.

5. Get Feedback from Others

Crafting a personal brand requires understanding how you're perceived. Would you deliver a speech without rehearsing it? Probably not. Yet many of us don't prepare how we present ourselves professionally.

Start by identifying how you want to be seen. Then ensure your actions align with that vision. Practice articulating your achievements in a way that feels natural, weaving them into conversations as part of your broader narrative.

However, self-awareness isn't enough, you need external feedback to identify gaps between your perception and reality. For that you need data and one of the best, albeit painful, ways to get it is to poll your audience with a formal or informal 360 evaluation. Conducting a formal or informal 360-degree evaluation offers valuable insights into how others view your strengths, challenges, and contributions. Identify gaps in your actual and desired perception and use this feedback constructively to refine your personal brand and communication style.

6. Authenticity: Trust Your Gut and Own Your Voice

Being intentional and setting clear goals are critical to effective communication and building a personal brand. However, authenticity is what binds your actions, words, and values into a cohesive narrative that others trust and respect.

Yet, authenticity often feels elusive, especially for women in leadership who navigate societal expectations and workplace biases. Overthinking, perfectionism, and the need for validation can often undermine our ability to show up as our true selves.

I experienced this firsthand when I was thrust into the biggest opportunity of my career: presenting our annual strategic plan and budget to the CEO and executive team. This was no ordinary presentation; it was my moment to showcase my leadership, my team's performance, and my ability to navigate high-stakes environments. I prepared meticulously, refining my slides and holding countless pre-meetings with key stakeholders. On presentation day, I confidently delivered my request for an additional $250K in budget, only to have my request completely ignored. Confused and deflated, I left the room, questioning where I went wrong.

The feedback I received was both enlightening and humbling. A VP told me, "You're not wrong, and I agree with your assessment, but you'll never get the budget. Everyone in that room is asking for something. Say something different." This was a turning point. Using the "5 Why's" method, I redefined my desired outcome, not to secure the budget but to gain approval for the strategic direction of my plan.

But it wasn't just my strategy that needed a reset; it was how I showed up. I realized I was tired of conforming to an image that wasn't me. I decided to be my authentic self, not the version I thought the room expected. The next day, I ditched my typical slacks and collared shirt for an outfit that reflected my personality: jeans, a pleated blouse, and hot pink heels. My presentation was no longer a plea or a proposal; it was a declaration. I presented my decisions as facts, outlining how I would execute the plan and allocate resources.

When I finished, there were no questions, and I left the room uncertain whether my bold approach had paid off. But by the end of the day, the CEO announced that my plan was the only one that met expectations, and I was invited to provide monthly updates to the executive team. Months later, without even asking, I was granted the additional budget.

That experience taught me that authenticity is career rocket fuel. When you align your words and actions with your true self, you create harmony between your intent and delivery. People trust and understand you because they see consistency, conviction, and capability.

Authenticity isn't just about being yourself, it's about aligning your actions, words, and values in a way that others can trust and respect. Overthinking and perfectionism may hold you back, but embracing your instincts and owning your voice can propel your career forward. When you lead with authenticity, your words carry weight because they are rooted in your values and experiences. Authentic communication isn't about perfection; it's about connection. After that presentation, I no longer felt the need to compete or prove myself. Instead, I focused on sharing the desired outcome.

Empower Your Voice: Effective Communication Strategies

Advocating for yourself as a woman leader in corporate environments requires confidence, authenticity, and the ability to position yourself as capable and influential. Think about this: How often do you dilute your voice in an effort to fit in or avoid criticism? What would change if you trusted your instincts and led with authenticity? The answer may be the key to unlocking your next big opportunity.

These strategies and techniques will help you communicate with impact and shape perceptions that align with your leadership goals:

Speak with Confidence and Precision

7. **Be Direct:** Avoid qualifying language like "I think" or "I feel or "not to sound arrogant" Instead, state your points assertively:
   "Based on my analysis, the most effective strategy is..."
   - **Control Your Tone:** Maintain a steady and authoritative tone, avoiding upward inflections that sound uncertain.

Use Data to Showcase Capability

8. Present measurable outcomes of your work to build credibility and emphasize your contributions:
   "Last quarter, I led a project that increased efficiency by 20%, saving the company $150,000."

- Tie your accomplishments to broader organizational goals, demonstrating alignment with company priorities.

Master the Art of Strategic Questions

9. Ask open-ended questions that reflect curiosity and leadership:
   "How can we align our team's objectives to better support the company's vision?"
   - Use probing questions to position yourself as a thoughtful decision-maker: *"What metrics should we prioritize to measure success on this initiative?"*

Establish Thought Leadership

10. Share insights and solutions in meetings to position yourself as a leader:
    "One approach we could consider is integrating cross-functional teams to accelerate progress."
    - Volunteer for visibility opportunities like presenting at team meetings or leading key discussions.

Build Authentic Relationships

11. Use active listening to understand stakeholders' needs and build trust.
    - Share both your personal and professional vision and values authentically, allowing others to see you as relatable and grounded.

Position Yourself as a Resource

12. Frame your expertise as beneficial to others:
    "If anyone needs support on analyzing metrics, let me know, I've worked on similar projects and would love to help."
    - Offer solutions rather than just highlighting problems to establish yourself as a problem-solver.

Conclusion: Embracing the Power of Your Voice

Advocating for yourself as a woman leader in corporate environments requires more than just knowing your worth, it demands clear intention, strategic communication, and unwavering authenticity. By defining your desired outcomes, seeking feedback to refine your personal brand, trusting your instincts to show up authentically, and using effective communication techniques to convey your impact, you can take control of your narrative.

Each of these principles builds upon the other, empowering you to navigate corporate spaces with confidence and purpose. The journey to self-advocacy is not without challenges, but the rewards are profound: increased visibility, trust, and the ability to shape your career on your terms. By integrating these strategies into your leadership approach, you can unlock opportunities, inspire others, and create a lasting legacy of influence and impact.

About the Author

Juwayriyah Hussain

Visionary Marketing Strategist | Builder of Brands

Champion for Women in Tech

Juwayriyah Hussein is a powerhouse in product marketing with more than two decades of experience shaping the future of technology. Her career spans the semiconductor, software, data center infrastructure, and artificial intelligence (AI) industries, where she has consistently turned complex ideas into compelling stories that resonate globally.

A proven architect of success, Juwayriyah has launched two startup tech companies from stealth mode to the spotlight and introduced over a dozen groundbreaking products at industry titans like Xilinx, Intel, AMD, and Altera. Her deep expertise in market research, strategic messaging, and pipeline development has translated into measurable impact, including growing customer bases from zero to tens of thousands in record time.

Juwayriyah is not just a marketer; she is a leader who thrives at the intersection of strategy and execution. Having managed diverse, global teams, she is known for fostering talent, building collaborative cultures, and guiding others to exceed their potential. This passion extends to her boutique fractional CMO agency, where she empowers companies across deep tech, AI, fashion, real estate, and software to craft bold, effective marketing strategies.

Beyond her impressive professional achievements, Juwayriyah's work reflects her dedication to inclusivity and empowerment. Her mission to create pathways for analytical, introverted women to advocate authentically for themselves stems from her own journey of balancing technical expertise with visionary leadership. She is passionate about equipping others with actionable tools to thrive in their careers and stand confidently in their worth.

Yet, for all her accolades, Juwayriyah finds her greatest joy in her personal life. As a devoted mother to two remarkable sons, she is committed to raising compassionate, thoughtful leaders who will leave a positive mark on the world.

Juwayriyah Hussein embodies what it means to lead with purpose, transform challenges into opportunities, and inspire others to reach for the extraordinary.

Contact Information:

Juwayriyah Hussain
Website: www.fmfc.us
Email: juwayriyah@fmfc.us
Social media: www.LinkedIn.com/in/juwayriyah

Chapter 11

Strengthen Your Network

Gaining Exposure Through Communication

Terri Barnes

It's not about who you know, but who knows you, and...

You've probably heard the quote "It's not about who you know, but who knows you." What if I added to the latter part "and how they feel about you."? Take a moment and think about where you are in your career right now. Are you feeling stuck, wondering why others seem to get opportunities that you know you're qualified for? Or maybe you're' doing well but sense that something's missing, that extra boost that could take you to the next level? I've been there, and I want to share with you what I've learned about creating your own opportunities through the power of authentic connections.

Imagine a defining moment in a career: A crowded conference room buzzes with anticipation as hundreds of leaders and executives await feedback on the company's strategic direction. While most colleagues shrink into their seats, hoping to avoid the spotlight, my colleague Keith (name changed) is called upon and rises with quiet confidence. His insights and compelling words cut through the silence, holding the room spellbound. One executive is so impressed that he reaches out to Keith personally after the meeting.

Fast-forward to today: Keith now leads an organization, reporting directly to that same executive. But this wasn't mere luck or perfect timing. Behind that pivotal moment lay years of deliberate effort. Keith had methodically built his reputation through consistent performance, authentic leadership, and a genuine commitment to others' success. When opportunity knocked, he was prepared to answer.

I understand the impatience of waiting for your breakthrough moment; I've often spent countless nights wondering when my time would come. But here's the encouraging truth: you can actively shape your future rather than leaving it to chance. This chapter will guide you through the art of intentional relationship building and show you how to leverage your network for meaningful exposure.

While the principles I'll share aren't complex, their power lies in consistent and purposeful application. Strong connections often exist within your current circle, but the key questions are: How well do these potential allies know your capabilities and character? Have you earned their trust? I firmly believe we're all here to help each other reach our destinations. The right connections can accelerate your journey toward your goals, but only if you invest in building and nurturing those relationships with authenticity and purpose.

Understanding Your Network Through Mentors and Sponsors

Let me share something that took me years to understand. Early in my career, I thought having a mentor was the golden ticket. Don't get me wrong, mentors are invaluable, and so are sponsors! However, their roles are different.

Mentors serve as trusted guides and advisors, drawing from their experience and expertise to help others navigate their personal and professional development. They provide invaluable support by sharing knowledge, offering constructive feedback, and assisting mentees to identify and work toward their goals. Let me paint a picture of what effective mentorship looks like:

A mentor's role:

- Serve as role models
- Demonstrate professional behavior and ethics
- Creating a safe space for mentees to learn
- Help bridge the gap between theory and practice
- Enable mentees to develop confidence and competence

Now, think of sponsors as your advocates, your champions, the people who have a seat at the table and fight for you when you're not in the room. They know your work; they believe in your work and capabilities. They trust that if they recommend you, you WILL perform. Let me paint a picture of what effective sponsorship looks like:

A sponsor's role:

- Advocate for you in high-level meetings where opportunities are discussed
- Put their corporate currency on the line to endorse you for key positions

- Intentionally create visibility for your work among decision-makers
- Provide strategic advice about organizational dynamics
- Provide you with a competitive advantage and amplify your already stellar performance

For my journey, it was key to knowing the difference between mentor and sponsor in my personal network web.

Understanding Your Network Web

Now that you understand the difference between a mentor and a sponsor, let's explore a powerful framework for visualizing and understanding your professional relationships: the Network Web.

Think of your professional network not as a simple list of contacts but as an intricate spider web, with you at the center. Each strand represents a connection – some thick and sturdy, others delicate and new. These strands stretch out in all directions, connecting you to people across different departments, industries, and even continents. Just as a spider carefully constructs its web, you've been building these connections throughout your career, perhaps without even realizing it.

Your Network Web extends far beyond your immediate professional circle. Picture concentric circles radiating outward from you. The innermost circle might include your daily colleagues, your direct supervisor, and immediate team members. The next circle could encompass people you interact with regularly but not daily, perhaps colleagues from other departments, clients, or vendors. Moving outward, you'll find former coworkers, industry peers you've' met at conferences, and professionals you've' connected with through various associations or groups.

But here's where it gets interesting: your Network Web isn't just about direct connections. Each person in your web has their own web of relationships and so on. When these webs intersect, they create powerful opportunities for connection and growth. Understanding your Network Web means to leverage your Network Web truly, start by mapping it out. Where are your strongest connections? Where might there be gaps? Which strands could use strengthening?

Understanding these dynamics helps you make strategic decisions about where to invest your networking energy. Perhaps you notice your web is strong within your current company but lacks connections in adjacent industries. Or maybe you realize you have many peers in your network but few senior-level connections who could serve as sponsors.

Remember, every professional interaction, no matter how small, has the potential to add a new strand to your web or strengthen an existing one. Every day is an interview. Your Network Web is a living, breathing entity that grows and evolves with your career. By understanding its structure and dynamics, you can more effectively nurture the relationships that will support your professional growth and equally important if not more, create opportunities for others within your network to thrive as well.

Exercise

Let's do something together right now. Grab a piece of paper, yes, actually grab one, I'll wait! Now, let's reflect on these questions (be honest with yourself; no one else needs to see this):

- Why do you want exposure? What drives this desire?
- What type of exposure would make the biggest difference in your career right now?
- Who are the right people who could help you get there? (Think big!)
- How would this exposure change your professional journey?
- What's really holding you back? Name those obstacles.

Now, let's visualize your network as a web page. Close your eyes for a moment and think about every person you've connected with professionally. Your current colleagues, yes, but go deeper, think about the person you chatted with at last year's conference, your old college roommate who is a CEO, maybe former project teammates, the executive who is now in operations now, even your child coach who happens to work in your industry. Think beyond work: community groups, religious organizations, sports teams, neighborhood connections, and parent networks. Don't forget past connections from previous jobs, education, or activities.

Your network is probably bigger than you realized, isn't it? Were some tucked away in the back of your mind?

Now, envision your network as an intricate web, each strand representing a connection to another person or group. The question is: How strong are these connections? Strong networks aren't just about quantity; they're about quality and depth of relationships. Connections can break easily if not fostered and cared for. Some break due to bad or negative interactions and those connections cannot be rebuilt, some call it burning bridges. Or maybe your web doesn't have many strings, only a few. Speaking from experience, sometimes it only takes a few to hold, but those few must make up for their lack of abundance, in strength, that comes from deepening those connections. This is where you look at your web and ask what can I do to strengthen these strings?

The Connection That Gave Me Exposure

When I became a global manager, my boss was a Vice President (VP) at that time. My very first year of reporting to her was challenging; however, I must admit it was the most rewarding because I learned so much about myself. She was a black savvy businesswoman who fought to attain her position; and let's be honest, she likely constantly fought to have her voice heard to get to her level as a black woman throughout the 80s, 90s, even up to this point in her career. Her tenacious drive and reputation for excellence set the tone for her leadership. She established ambitious targets for her team, and meeting these rigorous benchmarks wasn't optional, it was an expectation. In professional confrontations, she proved to be a formidable opponent, commanding thorough preparation and ironclad arguments from anyone who engaged with her, an art she was required to perfect to be successful.

When our weekly one-on-one meetings first began, I dedicated two hours to organizing my thoughts and anticipating her questions. As meeting time approached, my anxiety manifested physically: clammy palms, perspiration, and rising body temperature marked my journey down the hallway to her office. I learned to carry water, both for my tension-constricted throat and as a prop for strategic pauses. I knew she would challenge my thinking, that I may not have answers to her tough questions, or I would leave her office thinking, 'How am I going to achieve this directive she just gave me?' Our meetings felt intense.

Yet her fierce advocacy had an unexpected upside: once you earned her trust, she championed your cause with the same intensity. Her approach to performance reviews particularly resonated with me. "I'm going to tell my boss what my performance appraisal score should be," she would say, "and they can explain to me why I shouldn't get it." I admired this bold stance, especially given that annual raises hung in the balance, and it exemplified her fearless nature. Her fighting spirit, combined with extensive professional connections forged through years of dedication, consistently delivered results. Through sheer determination and strategic networking, she had built an impressive sphere of influence that extended far beyond her immediate role.

Although the first year was a struggle for me, it was the time I grew the most, personally and professionally. During the first few months under her leadership, she unveiled her strategic vision for my team's future. While I grasped the merits of her proposed direction, I harbored concerns about our organizational readiness. The implementation would require substantial groundwork, particularly IT support to consolidate applications across more than 40 sites, and extensive process alignment to ensure a seamless transition. My conservative estimate placed this preparatory phase at two years minimum.

When I attempted to outline these challenges and propose a roadmap forward, she suggested that I needed to think bigger and not be defensive about my scope. The characterization stunned me. "Defensive" is so far from my typical demeanor that I sought specific examples, hoping to understand her perspective. Rather than becoming defensive about being called defensive, I approached it with curiosity and openness.

However, I perceived at that moment she had already drawn her conclusions. In her view, my analytical approach to implementation challenges represented resistance to change rather than strategic foresight. I felt she interpreted my systematic breakdown of obstacles as an unwillingness to embrace transformation.

Later that day, seeking perspective, I reached out to a former boss-turned-friend. Her response was telling: "Terri, she clearly doesn't know who you are." Those words captured the essence of our misalignment, a fundamental misreading of my professional character and intentions. I eventually realized that my boss was not trying to bring me anxiety or offend me. Her desire was to push me outside my comfort zone and recognize the possibilities and strengths I possessed. Fast-forward to today, we have an amazing relationship, value each other's authenticity, and she is now my mentor again. She was one of the best managers I've had in my career.

Although we started off rocky in our dynamic, I had to learn how to strengthen my web with my boss. Why was this important? Eventually, she was key in giving me exposure to her peers, other Vice Presidents, and her boss, a Senior Vice President in the company. She gave me projects and provided opportunities that put me in front of these senior leaders, not once but multiple times; and those opportunities led me to others.

Prior to this role, my professional network had been entirely self-built through strategic yet organic relationship building. I seized natural opportunities for connection, striking up conversations at company picnics, sharing elevator rides, or extending invitations for tea or lunch. These initial touchpoints often blossomed into deeper professional relationships. My established network partners frequently became bridges, connecting me with key stakeholders who could advance my projects and initiatives.

This grassroots approach to relationship building, while effective, required patience and persistent effort.

Before my VP's instrumental role in elevating my visibility, securing access to senior leadership had been a persistent challenge. Through navigating this complex dynamic, I discovered three fundamental principles that transformed my path to greater organizational exposure:

1. Be Authentic
2. Have Genuine Interest In Others
3. Communicate, Communicate, Communicate!

By using these three concepts or intentions, sometimes in tandem, I was able to get more exposure by strengthening the connection I had with my "not so easily shaken" and challenging boss. I knew I wanted more exposure to leaders within the company to help develop my career and develop partnerships. I learned that by setting these intentions with my boss, instead of fighting me, she fought for me.

Intention 1: Be Authentic, "There is No Other You!"

In a twist of fate, before our formal reporting relationship began, I had actually chosen my boss as my mentor. Her fierce spirit and unwavering determination drew me to her, qualities which contrasted sharply with my own approach at the time. While my natural inclination favored a softer side and measured responses to conflict, I recognized the value in her bold methodology. Though I never shied away from confrontation, my approach was markedly different from her direct style.

During our mentorship, she shared invaluable insights about assertiveness and timing. One piece of wisdom particularly resonated: before speaking up, ask yourself three questions: "Should this be said? Should this be said right now? And should this be said by me?" This framework became a cornerstone of my conflict management approach, helping me navigate disagreements with strategic precision while maintaining my authentic style.

Attempting to emulate her directness, I sent an uncharacteristically forceful email. The response was equally tense: he would address my "demands" when time permitted. Recognizing the damage to our previously cordial relationship, I quickly arranged a face-to-face meeting to explain my out-of-character behavior. His response, "This email didn't feel like Terri," confirmed the importance of staying true to one's authentic leadership style. This situation is where I started truly discovering my authentic self.

Being true to my authentic self, emerged as the cornerstone of my professional success. While I gradually developed a more direct communication style, I did so in a way that remained true to my core values. When I shared the peer interaction incident with my boss during my year-end review, she acknowledged the effectiveness of my collaborative approach, though different from her own style, she had come to respect it. Through observing her interactions with others, I came to respect her approach; she was being authentic to who she was.

A turning point emerged when I stopped trying to win her approval and focused on exhibiting my unique strengths, something she had been trying to get me to do from the beginning, honestly. I leveraged my engineering background to comprehensively analyze my team's resource allocation, workload gaps, and strategic solutions. This data-driven approach, combined with my natural collaborative style, finally bridged our disconnect. She began to see the full spectrum of my capabilities and how my authentic leadership style could drive results.

This transformative experience clearly revealed a profound professional truth: when we bring our genuine selves to work, we cultivate deeper trust and forge stronger connections with colleagues. Success in leadership doesn't come from imitating others' management styles or trying to fit into predetermined molds. Instead, it emerges from recognizing and refining our unique strengths while maintaining openness to growth and evolution.

Intention 2: Have a Genuine Interest in Others; Help Both of You Win!

The true essence of professional networking extends far beyond simple transactional relationships. When we embrace the mindset that we're all on parallel journeys of growth and development, helping each other reach our destinations becomes natural and meaningful. Think of networking as a vast tapestry of interconnected paths, where each intersection represents an opportunity to support someone else's journey while advancing our own.

However, the depth of these professional connections depends heavily on our ability to demonstrate authentic interest in others. This means going beyond surface-level interactions to understand what truly motivates our colleagues, what challenges they face, and what aspirations drive them forward. By investing time to discover what matters most to others, whether it's their professional goals, personal projects, or the causes they champion, they create bonds that transcend typical workplace relationships. These deeper connections not only enrich our professional experience but also create a robust support system where mutual growth and success become inevitable outcomes.

And not just using this knowledge to benefit you but because you have a genuine interest in helping them reach their goals and desires. The last thing you want is for someone in your network to think you are using them just to succeed for yourself. No one wants to be used.

I recall when I first started my professional career. I was fresh out of college and went to work in a manufacturing facility, made up of mostly male blue-collar employees, many of them had more than 10-15+ years of experience. The one person I knew at the site, gave me the best piece of advice that I carried on throughout my career. He said "Before you're given a project or really start your role, Terri, go and learn. Learn the operation, the processes, but most importantly learn the people." It's commonly understood that when you get into a new role, you should learn the processes and the work being executed by talking to the people who perform the work; but you would be surprised how many leaders come into a new role with their own "agenda" and don't attempt to understand what is truly happening in the organization they have been asked to lead.

After getting this piece of advice, I took it to heart. I began sitting with lead operators, subject matter experts, supervisors and everyone in between. Not only did I learn their processes and what they do, but I learned about them as a person. I found out about their lives, family, and interests. Not only did I learn, but I showed genuine interest.

I had worked on some small projects here and there for the first 2 months, but my first big project came 3 months into the job. I was tasked to improve our site's inventory process. I was super excited.

Utilizing my skills in Lean Manufacturing and what I learned about inventory, I worked with the inventory specialist each day, respecting her job, her experience, and conveyed the importance of the changes. It's important to note that because of the relationship I built with the inventory specialist, this person supported me and my project. Because I cared, we ended up freeing up over $1M dollars in cash, partnering together. And to think, much of the success of the project was because we built a deeper connection that surpassed work. I strengthened my network through this one connection. Based on the success of this major project, I received a similar project focusing on improving the receiving warehouse's process. Using the approach of deepening the connections, when I proposed my improvements and changes, a member on the team said, "Terri, I don't agree with your proposal. I don't think this will work, but because it's YOU, I'll do it." Wow! I had a chance to implement my ideas because it was "me" and they trusted "me".

Now let's be honest, we all have a job to do. It's not always possible to spend weeks with a person or team. You will have to find that balance and how best you can deepen those connections. It could be through spending time or even remembering that they had an important event over the weekend and asking them about it. We as humans want to be heard and when someone shows genuine interest in you as a person, they remember that.

Importantly, I also shared aspects of my own life, which helped build trust and authenticity in relationships.

What emerges can be a meaningful connection where both parties genuinely support each other's personal and professional growth, creating a more enriching work experience.

Intention 3: Communicate, "It Builds Trust"

We've all heard that communication is key and it's true. No matter what type of relationship you are nourishing, you must communicate for that relationship to flourish. You may be thinking – this is an easy one. However, one can believe they're communicating, but communication isn't really happening. Realize that communication is a two-way street with talking and listening and not listening to respond. You can do your job, and your performance speaks for itself, but if you do not know how to communicate by understanding your audience and communicating what they need or want to know, you may be perceived as not a great communicator.

There is a communication model that I like to share used by the National Communication Association. This model, the Transactional Model of Communication, depicts how we are the sender and receivers of a message, how we must encode and decode messages through different channels while recognizing there may be noise that has a potential to disrupt the message. This is a great example of how communication works through talking and listening.

Transactional Model of Communication

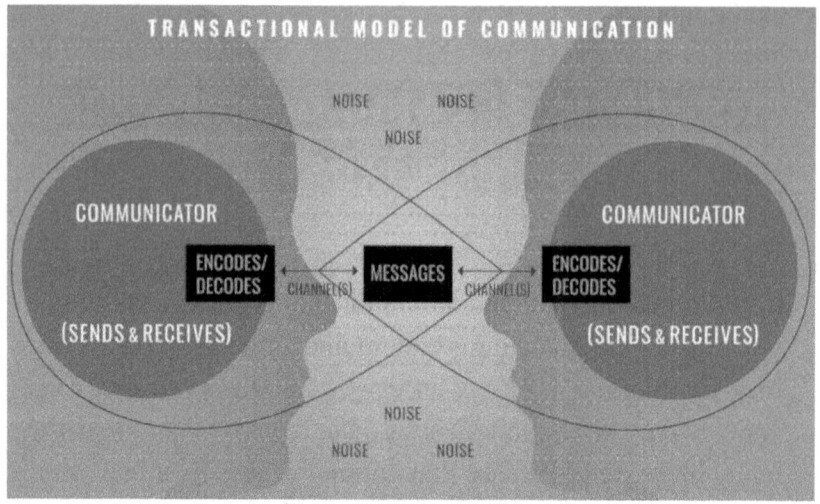

Conclusion

"Your network is more than a collection of professional contacts - it's a living ecosystem of relationships that can elevate your career when nurtured with intention and authenticity. By remaining true to your unique professional identity, demonstrating a sincere interest in others' success, and maintaining open communication channels, you create a web of support that can withstand challenges and propel you toward your goals. Remember, every interaction is an opportunity to strengthen these connections, and every relationship holds the potential for mutual growth. The path to increased visibility and influence begins with understanding that meaningful exposure comes not from merely being seen but from being known, trusted, and valued for your authentic contributions. As you move forward, focus on building relationships that reflect your genuine character while creating value for others. Your network's strength lies not in its size, but in the depth and quality of the connections you forge."

About the Author

Terri Barnes

Global Senior Leader and ERG Leader, Oil & Gas, Film and Theatre Actress

Terri received a Bachelor of Science Degree in Engineering Management from Missouri Science & Technology (formally University of Missouri-Rolla). As a kid, she never wanted to be an engineer but to pursue acting. Instead, Terri received a track scholarship at an Engineering school where she completed internships at Fortune 500 companies such as Walt Disney World and Anheuser-Busch. After graduating, Terri began working as a Lean Manufacturing Engineer for 3M Company. She earned a Lean Six Sigma Green Belt certification. She then led the implementation of a lean management system for the site, which helped her truly understand the details of how a management system works and deepened her belief that everyone has a role to play in Quality.

Terri's career path took her to Houston, Texas where she became a Quality Supervisor for Goodman Manufacturing, overseeing a team of Quality Inspectors and gaining insight into Quality compliance and standards. After her supervisory role, Terri transitioned to Oil and Gas starting as a Process Quality Engineer, working on improvement projects. She then stepped into a global role facilitating the development of process mapping. She was eventually promoted to a position as North America Quality Management System (QMS) Manager where she was responsible for implementing QMS industry standards and managing internal audits. After her success in this role, she advanced to Global Quality Systems Senior Manager, where she manages a Global QMS team and is responsible for managing Quality Systems & Applications and Quality Reporting & Analysis. Terri also still continues to support her passion for the arts, performing on stage as well as roles in television commercials, short films, and feature films. Terri currently resides in Houston, TX.

Contact Information:
Terri Barnes
Website: Terrirenee-actorwebsite.com
Email: Terri2barnes@gmail.com
Social Media: https://www.linkedin.com/in/terri-barnes-12b922138

EXPOSURE

POSITIONING YOURSELF FOR OPPORTUNITY WITH INTENTION

Too often, leaders are thrust into positions of influence without the necessary exposure, relationships, or preparation to navigate them effectively. Others spend years excelling behind the scenes, believing their work alone will earn them recognition, only to find themselves overlooked. True career acceleration requires more than talent, it requires intentional exposure, and the ability to be seen before the opportunity arrives.

Redefining leadership means rejecting the idea that success happens by chance and instead embracing the power of positioning. Visibility is not just about personal advancement, it's about creating access for others, using your platform to elevate new voices, and ensuring that leadership pipelines reflect a broader range of talent and perspectives. Leaders who understand the power of exposure don't just build their own success, they cultivate opportunities for those who follow, shaping the next generation of leadership. In the chapters ahead, our authors explore the importance of cultivating meaningful visibility, knowing when to step forward, when to embrace the waiting season, and how to ensure that when your moment arrives, you are fully prepared to lead. Your leadership impact should never be left to chance, own your exposure, control your narrative, and ensure that when opportunity knocks, decision-makers already know your name.

Chapter 12

Thrust Into Leadership

From Uncertain Teen to International Influence

Dr. Tabatha Russell

"Leadership is not about being the best; it's about making others better through your influence and example." **– Dr. Tabatha Russell**

The Call to Lead: A Journey of Unlikely Beginnings

Leadership often calls upon us in the most unexpected moments; sometimes, those moments find us wholly unprepared. For me, that call came at the tender age of 17, a pivotal time when many are still searching for their identity and purpose. I wasn't chosen because of my age, credentials, or extraordinary skills, I was chosen because I was the senior-most person by tenure, not age. Yet, in that baptism by fire, one that forced me to tap into reserves of resilience, adaptability, and courage I didn't yet know I possessed. I discovered resilience, adaptability, and courage that would become the foundation of my leadership philosophy.

That trial by leadership became the foundation of my philosophy, a blend of perseverance, authenticity, and the unwavering pursuit of excellence. It shaped the leader I would become, paving the way for my journey to becoming an internationally recognized speaker, author, coach, and investor.

Through sleepless nights and the intense crucible of day-and-night training sessions, I pieced together all of the leadership styles, eventually forging my own. My story is one of transformation: from a young, reluctant leader to a savvy, purposeful, and uncommon trailblazer.

In this journey, I'll share the lessons, insights, and strategies that helped me redefine leadership, not just for myself but for others seeking to embrace their unique potential. Together, we'll explore what it truly means to lead boldly, authentically, and with intention.

I Was Being Exposed

The fluorescent lights hummed softly above me as I stood in the breakroom, barely old enough to vote but somehow responsible for leading a team of people older, and, in many ways, more experienced than me. I had just been promoted, not because of my exceptional skills or any groundbreaking achievements, but because I was the "longest-tenured" employee at 17. In our small organization, that title came with responsibilities I wasn't sure I was ready for.

I can still feel the nervous energy that buzzed in my chest as I prepared for my first team meeting. My hands trembled slightly, and my voice wavered when I introduced myself as the new leader. The room was quiet, but their expressions said it all: *She's just a kid.*

They weren't wrong, I *was* just a kid. But I was also fiercely determined to prove them wrong.

What followed was a crash course in leadership, one that no amount of seniority could prepare me for. The team I inherited was disorganized, unmotivated, and skeptical of me from day one. I learned quickly that leadership wasn't about issuing orders or clinging to policies. It was about building trust, creating connections, and providing clarity.

There was no manual to guide me, no mentor to lean on. My training consisted of fragmented lessons during the day and sleepless nights trying to figure out what worked. There were moments of triumph when everything seemed to click, and there were plenty of moments when I stumbled, unsure if I was making progress. But through it all, I refused to stop learning. Every misstep taught me something. Every challenge strengthened me.

That breakroom became the first stage of my leadership journey. It wasn't glamorous or easy, but it was the crucible that forged the foundation of the leader I am today.

From Proving Myself to Empowering Others

The turning point in my leadership journey came on a particularly chaotic day when everything that could go wrong seemed to happen at once. A major deadline loomed, my team was visibly frustrated, and I felt like I was on the verge of tears. I didn't have the answers, and the weight of trying to hold everything together was overwhelming. That night, I stayed late, searching for clarity in leadership books and articles.

One phrase stopped me in my tracks: *"Leadership is not about you; it's about them and us as a team."*

It was like a lightning bolt. Up until that moment, I had been so consumed with proving myself, trying to look capable, confident, and in control, that I had overlooked the real solution: focusing on my team. Leadership wasn't about me; it was about empowering everyone to succeed.

The next day, I approached my team differently. Instead of dictating tasks, I sought their input. I listened more and talked less. I encouraged collaboration and celebrated every small win. Slowly but surely, I could feel the dynamic beginning to shift. The team could sense I was no longer out for myself. Trust replaced skepticism, and the team started to move as a cohesive unit.

It wasn't just a feeling; it was backed by evidence. I later learned that according to a study by Gallup, teams led by highly engaged leaders are 21% more productive. I saw this in real-time as my team grew more cohesive, motivated, and resilient.

That experience was the moment I understood the transformative power of authentic leadership. It's not about standing at the front and demanding results, it's about walking alongside your team, equipping them with the tools, trust, and confidence they need to excel. That lesson became a cornerstone of my leadership philosophy. These foundational insights have shaped the leader I am today, and they serve as guiding principles for the lessons I've learned along the way. Let me share the leadership strategies that have not only defined my journey but also empowered those I lead.

1. The Power of Self-Investment: Leading Through Self-Discovery

Leadership begins within. We often ignore our own personal development for the sake of delivering results. But the true transformation starts with an investment in yourself, a commitment to understanding your strengths, values, and blind spots. It's a journey of self-discovery and growth that requires intentionality, persistence, and courage. For me, it began with certifications, mentorships, conferences, and reflective practices. These investments sharpened my skills and built the foundation for a leadership style rooted in authenticity and purpose.

Self-investment has provided some of the greatest returns imaginable. While financial success is a welcome byproduct, the true reward is the satisfaction of watching those I lead reach their potential. When I show up as my best self, I'm better equipped to inspire, empower, and uplift my team and clients.

Leadership isn't about perfection but about continuous improvement. Here are the strategies that have shaped me into the leader I am today:

- **Embrace Vulnerability:** Authenticity builds trust. Sharing struggles and showing humanity inspires loyalty and connection.
- **Cultivate Self-Awareness:** Leadership is as much about knowing your blind spots as it is about leveraging your strengths. Every day is an excellent

opportunity to be 1% better. Plans that remain unimplemented will always fail, so take action.
- **Prioritize Communication:** Listen actively and speak with intention. Seek feedback regularly and ensure those around you feel valued and heard.
- **Lead with Vision:** Align your team with a compelling purpose. A shared vision fosters unity and commitment.
- **Invest in Development:** Empower your team through growth opportunities, knowing that as they rise, so will you.
- **Adapt and Innovate:** Leadership evolves. Stay flexible and open to refining your approach.

When you take the time to understand who you are and invest in your growth, you create a solid foundation that anchors you through life's storms. This clarity allows you to navigate challenges, seize opportunities, and lead with purpose. Leadership isn't a destination; it's a journey, and the first step is investing in yourself.

Investing in Myself to Impact Others: The Ripple Effect of Leadership

Fast-forward 30 years, and the lessons I learned in those early days of leadership remain foundational. Today, as a Chief Executive Officer of Inside Inspired Women Consulting Global, I know that my role goes far beyond setting goals and achieving targets. It's about equipping my team with the tools, resources, and encouragement they need to thrive, not just professionally but personally as well. It's about creating an environment where staff and clients feel valued, appreciated, and understood.

2. Equipping My Team: Empowering Growth and Success

One of the most significant shifts in my leadership approach has been the emphasis on equipping my team for success. Leadership transcends task delegation or setting expectations; it requires creating an environment where individuals can thrive through meaningful development.

1. **Comprehensive Training:** Every new hire undergoes an immersive onboarding process that ensures they understand their role and the company's mission, vision, and values. Beyond onboarding, I prioritize ongoing training tailored to their specific needs and aspirations.
2. **Individual Development Plans:** Personalized growth plans are integral to my approach. By aligning each team member's career objectives with targeted development opportunities, such as leadership training, skill enhancement, or mentorship, I ensure they have the tools to excel.
3. **Empowerment and Autonomy:** Creativity and innovation flourish in environments of trust. I encourage my team to take ownership of their roles, providing guidance when necessary while avoiding the pitfalls of micromanagement.

4. **Mental Health and Well-being:** True leadership prioritizes humanity alongside productivity. I create a supportive space where individuals feel valued and cared for through wellness programs, mental health resources, and flexible work arrangements.

These practices have cultivated a culture of empowerment, one where team members feel equipped to excel, take charge of their professional growth, and contribute meaningfully to collective success.

3. Creating a Culture of Appreciation: The Heart of Leadership

The heart of leadership is people. Over the years, I've learned that when people feel genuinely appreciated and valued, they perform at their best. Here's how I've embedded a culture of appreciation into my leadership style:

1. **Celebrate All Success:** Whether it's a milestone, a completed project, or a small win, I make it a point to recognize and celebrate achievements. From handwritten notes to team shoutouts, appreciation is part of our DNA.
2. **Foster Open Communication:** Feedback is a two-way street. I've cultivated an environment where dialogue flows freely, ensuring that every voice is heard. Listening to my team and clients not only validates their contributions but also drives meaningful improvement.
3. **Prioritize Relationships:** rust and loyalty are built on authentic connections. By understanding the

unique needs, goals, and concerns of both my staff and clients, I create relationships that go beyond transactions, fostering deep and lasting bonds.

Appreciation is not just an occasional act but a foundational element of effective leadership. By embedding gratitude and recognition into daily practices, I've created an atmosphere where individuals feel valued, motivated, and empowered to excel.

The Ripple Effect: Redefining Leadership for Generational Impact

The investment I made in myself decades ago continues to ripple outward. By prioritizing self-growth, I've redefined leadership as a legacy of empowerment, innovation, and transformation. It's not just about personal success; it's about elevating those around me to achieve their fullest potential. Investing in yourself is a powerful act that yields dividends far greater than any monetary reward. It establishes a foundation of trust, respect, and loyalty that transcends every interaction and relationship.

My leadership journey has been punctuated by moments of redefinition. Early in my career, I learned to embrace vulnerability as strength, speaking up even when I felt uncertain. In my first leadership role at 17, I was confronted with challenges that required resilience and adaptability. Those early lessons taught me that great leaders aren't born; they are forged through challenges and triumphs. These moments of courage not only solidified my values but also inspired trust and loyalty within my teams. I realized that leadership wasn't just about guiding others; it was about creating an environment where others felt safe to lead themselves.

Today, I stand as a testament to the power of persistence and self-belief. As an internationally recognized speaker, best-selling author, transformational coach, and successful investor, I've built an empire dedicated to helping others unlock their potential and embrace their unique leadership style. But it all began with a commitment to self-investment and the willingness to redefine leadership as an act of service and empowerment.

Lessons in Resilience and Self-Discovery

Leadership is a journey, not a destination. It's about growth, adaptability, and the courage to lead with authenticity. Every experience, whether triumphant or challenging, has shaped me into the serial business owner and strategic leader I am today. Life is an incredible teacher, and I've learned to embrace the lessons hidden in every setback and victory. From navigating the complexities of adulthood to stepping into high-stakes leadership roles, each moment has strengthened my ability to think strategically, adapt quickly, and lead with purpose.

The cornerstone of my growth has been the power of self-discovery. When you take the time to understand who you are, your strengths, values, and even blind spots, you create a foundation that anchors you through life's storms. There were moments when doubt crept in and challenges felt insurmountable, but resilience reminded me that I could navigate through anything. This clarity gave me the courage to take risks, seize opportunities, and build a legacy of lasting impact.

When taught and practiced with intention, leadership becomes a boundless force for success. It's not about power or position; it's about guiding others toward a shared vision while remaining anchored in your purpose. With resilience, self-discovery, and an unwavering commitment to growth, the possibilities for success are limitless. Leadership done right doesn't just elevate you, it uplifts everyone connected to your mission.

As you reflect on this chapter, consider the following questions:

1. What leadership challenges have you faced, and how did you overcome them?
2. How can you embrace vulnerability and authenticity in your leadership style?
3. What steps can you take today to empower and inspire those you lead?

Remember that leadership is not defined by age, title, or tenure. It's about influence, impact, and the ability to inspire others to greatness. The journey may not always be easy, but it is always worth it.

Gratitude: The Anchor of Leadership

I wouldn't trade my journey for anything in the world because every challenge, triumph, and lesson has deepened my love for leadership. The process of becoming a leader was far from smooth, but it was in those moments of struggle that I discovered my true strength and purpose. Leadership taught me how to navigate uncertainty, connect with people on a meaningful level, and rise to challenges with resilience. It wasn't just about becoming a leader; it was about learning to love responsibility, growth, and the profound impact leadership brings.

Of course, there were moments when I wanted to throw in the towel. Leadership can be overwhelming, and it's easy to mumble, grumble, and question the path forward. But through those moments, I learned that gratitude changes everything. My perspective shifted when I focused on the privilege to influence and inspire rather than the pressures of the role. Gratitude doesn't erase challenges but equips you to face them with grace and optimism.

Gratitude has been the cornerstone of my leadership philosophy. It reminds me to celebrate progress, even when perfection feels elusive. It encourages me to view obstacles as opportunities and value the people who support and challenge me. Through these practices, I've discovered a deeper appreciation for the journey, not just the milestones, but the everyday moments that shape us into the leaders we're meant to be.

Leadership, at its core, is about leaving a legacy of growth and empowerment. I hope this chapter inspires you to embrace your own leadership journey with courage, resilience, and gratitude. Let's create ripples of impact that uplift not only ourselves but everyone around us.

What's Next or, Better Yet, Who's Next?

Enough about me and my journey, what about you? Leadership isn't confined to a title or position; it's a mindset and a way of life. The question is, how will you take what you've read in this chapter and apply it to your own journey? Are you ready to embrace the challenges and opportunities that come with leadership? Whether you're leading a team, a family, or even just yourself, this is your moment to step into your potential and begin shaping the legacy you want to leave behind.

What inspires you about the stories you've just read? Is it the resilience to persevere through challenges, the determination to grow, or the commitment to invest in yourself? Take a moment to reflect on your own journey. What lessons can you draw from your experiences, and how can you use them to move forward? Remember, leadership isn't about having all the answers; it's about being willing to ask the right questions to learn, adapt, and grow. The key to success lies in your ability to harness the power of self-discovery and resilience to create a vision that inspires not only yourself but also those around you.

Now it's time to go to work. Start by identifying one area of your life where you can take ownership and lead with intention. It might be as simple as committing to personal growth or as bold as stepping into a new role or responsibility. Leadership begins with small, consistent actions that align with your vision. Think about the strategies shared in this chapter and how they can be customized to fit your unique situation. What steps will you take today to invest in yourself and create a solid foundation for the storms of life?

Don't underestimate the impact you can have. Leadership taught right has infinite possibilities for success, and you have everything you need to succeed within you. Surround yourself with people who challenge and uplift you, and don't be afraid to seek guidance or mentorship when needed. As you step into your role as a leader, remember that every experience, good or bad, is shaping you into the person you're meant to become.

Your story is still being written, and the possibilities are endless. Let this chapter serve as a call to action, a reminder that leadership is about more than titles or achievements, it's about making a difference. So, combine what you've learned here with your unique gifts and talents, and create a life and legacy you'll be proud of. The world is waiting for your leadership, voice, and vision. Now go to work and make it happen!

About the Author
Dr. Tabatha Russell

International Keynoter l Best-Selling Author l Financial Expert

"Take ownership by being the CEO of your life through transforming your mindset. You always see it before you can be or build it. Change your life through mastering your vision."

– Dr. Tabatha Russell

Dr. Tabatha Russell is a highly sought-after keynote speaker, best-selling author, and financial expert. She is arguably one of the most empowering, entertaining, and enthusiastic voices in transformational speaking today. Leveraging over 20 years of professional experience in the financial literacy industry, Dr. Tabatha is on a mission to train corporate and collegiate audiences to transform their relationship with their money so they can unapologetically permit themselves to experience the financial freedom, stability, independence, and security they deserve.

Affectionately known as the "Money Makeover Mogul," Dr. Tabatha has become the leading authority on financial empowerment and creating environments that foster success. She challenges clients to unapologetically use their life experience and expertise to live the 6-figure life of their dreams. She mentors passionately, guiding them to transition from employee to CEO of their life, business, and legacy.

Her extensive leadership expertise has landed her on major corporate stages across the United States, and her exceptional skills have allowed her to deliver keynotes to some of the most prominent corporate organizations in the industry. Dr. Tabatha has delivered heart-stirring keynote speeches on live and virtual international stages for large audiences, including Dr. Shawn Fair's Leadership Experience Tour, Finances Leadership Conference, 43rd Sisterhood Global Conference, and the Scars to Stripes Conference, to name a few.

Dr. Tabatha is a compelling thought leader who champions the empowerment of women around the world, providing opportunities to build courage, confidence, and connections through workshops, resources, education, and coaching. In line with her passion for helping women succeed, Dr. Tabatha founded Inside Inspired Women LLC™, a global company focused on equipping savvy business-women with skills and strategies to level up their price points and create multiple income streams to live the life of their dreams. She is the author of the bestselling book *I Divorced My Money and Married My Mindset*, a financial guide designed to challenge readers' thoughts about money.

Recognized as an influential figure, Dr. Tabatha holds three doctorate degrees and boasts a two-decade career as a corporate professional. She is a Certified Master Coach, Serial Entrepreneur, and Business and Life Strategist.

Dr. Tabatha is a visionary who has been recognized with numerous certifications and awards for her leadership, commitment, and contributions to her community and the next generation. Her work has been featured on prominent media platforms such as ABC, NBC, FOX, and CBS, talk shows, radio, and podcasts, and in leading newspapers and magazines, including *Shoutout Atlanta Magazine*, *Speakers Magazine*, and *Tap-In Magazine*, among others.

Contact Information:

Email: support@drtabathrussell.com
Website: https://DrTabathaRussell.com
Instagram: https://www.instagram.com/iamdrtabatha
Facebook: https://www.facebook.com/IamDrTabatha
LinkedIn: https://www.linkedin.com/in/tabatharussell

Chapter 13

Intentional Exposure

Embrace Your Wait; Timing is Everything...

Stephanie Johnson

"Trust the wait. Embrace the Beauty of Becoming. Everything comes to you at the perfect time. When nothing is certain, anything is possible."

~ Mandy Hale

Introduction

In a world that celebrates instant gratification, where same-day delivery and high speed everything has become the norm, we've forgotten a fundamental truth: some of life's most profound transformations require us to wait. Like a butterfly in its chrysalis or a seed beneath winter soil, periods of seeming stillness often mask the most powerful changes. This paradox – that waiting itself can be an active, transformative process – challenges our modern instincts. Yet those who learn to embrace their seasons of waiting often discover something extraordinary: these intervals aren't merely empty spaces between events, but rather rich territories of becoming.

Through this exploration, we'll discover how mastering the art of waiting can transform our experience of time itself, turning what might feel like life's holding patterns into opportunities for deep personal growth. When we truly understand that timing is everything, we begin to see our waiting periods not as obstacles, but as essential parts of our journey.

What Do You Do In The Face Of Uncertainty?

Choose to create. Choose to keep taking steps towards the vision of you that no one else sees. Of course, the journey will be filled with unexpected twists and turns, but if you remain persistent, you will ultimately bloom for all the world to see. You are worth the pursuit. Trust me when I tell you that you already have within you the resilience to overcome any obstacles that show up on your way to becoming the leader you desire to be. But here's the best-kept secret. There is no need to rush. Allow your journey to be just as extraordinary as the arrival. Let it unfold like a magnificent best-selling book. Because your story is the greatest one you will ever tell or share with the world. So, embrace your wait fully. If you think about it, the most majestic moments in our lives are all about the waiting prelude to your wedding day, the countdown to your high school or college graduation. And one of the most remarkable waiting periods: a mom preparing to give birth to the love of her life growing inside her womb. Just think about it. If her baby were to arrive too soon, there would be many setbacks and possible complications.

Birth, like all special moments where anticipation is the ultimate high, serves as a constant reminder that timing is everything. Embracing your wait is about recognizing and accepting that you are a life T.R.A.I.N.E.E. on a path to fulfilling your destiny. And when the time is right, you'll be ready for exposure. You'll be prepared for the world to know and see you without filters or fluff, unafraid to stand in all your God-given glory and own it. Being exposed at the right time is when all of the pieces of your life fall into place exactly as they should because what is meant to be will be. Timing is everything. Embrace your wait and the extraordinary gift of being a student of life while the seeds of greatness God stored inside of you grow through life's trials, tribulations, and unexpected situations. Ultimately, you will bloom if you stay the course and keep training. When the fruits of your greatness are ripe, that's when you're ready to be exposed to the world so that others can see your light; be strengthened and sustained by your light until they, too, are ready to shine. Let's explore the T.R.A.I.N.E.E. framework to fulfill your destiny.

There is no growth without transition. Transition is the time and space we need to move from one state of being to another. My path to becoming the founder and CEO of a public relations consulting firm has been filled with many highs and lows, but each aspect has taught me something I needed to learn, even when I didn't know I needed a lesson at all. That's why I wouldn't go back and change a single thing. I've learned to trust God's timing. Every trial and test I endured was preparing me for my rebirth. To say I love the work I enjoy now would be an understatement. My clients are like family. My team is like family, and I enjoy the freedom of creating a beautiful environment for all of us to thrive together. When my team wins, I win; when my clients win, I win. When I'm meeting with my team or clients, it feels like sacred moments with my God-given tribe.

I also love having the freedom to prioritize my family and service to my community and church. I'm in the place I dreamed of being countless times before I arrived. And though I have the title of CEO, it doesn't define me. I used to believe work titles held a special meaning foolishly. And I've had some pretty impressive ones throughout my career, including Vice President of Enterprise Communications for the American Cancer Society, Vice President of

Communications and Product Strategies for the American Medical Association, Vice President of Communications for Advocate Aurora Health (Formerly Advocate Health Care), Segment Producer for Good Morning America, Researcher, and Associate Producer for World News Tonight with Peter Jennings, Television Anchor, and Reporter for the Hearst Corporation.

I was proud to hold every one of these positions, but I realize now none of the roles ever defined me, and no single role ever will. I am a soul who loves to love, and I share the love inside me with the world through writing and storytelling. I got my love for reading from my mommy. Her downtime was spent curling up on her favorite recliner, reading or doing crossword puzzles. I remember watching how peaceful and happy she looked, reading her favorite books, and how her face beamed with a big, gorgeous smile when she came up with the missing letters to finish her favorite crossword puzzle without cheating. I wanted to be just like her, a homemaker with a house full of children. There were eight of us. I never imagined as a little girl that my passion for reading and storytelling would take me from the tiny town in Mississippi where I grew up to so many extraordinary places.

I also never considered the value so many people placed on "fancy work titles" and the zip codes where you live or grew up as measurements of your worth. When I held executive positions at highly regarded companies, I was regularly called on for favors and invited to posh events. I rubbed shoulders with some of the world's wealthiest and most influential leaders. I felt loved. I thought I had many people in my corner that I could count on. But it was all an illusion. You want to know how I knew even back then… because I felt like an imposter. I was an executive leader too afraid to be brutally honest when other leaders crossed integrity lines and values I hold dear. I stayed silent because I was too scared to let go of the status that the positions garnered me, to tell the truth, and to let the chips fall where they may. I said I trusted God, but I didn't act like it. Still, I prayed, cried, and asked God for strength to do the right things, the noble things. I was ready to evolve, but I didn't know how. Life has a funny way of nudging you toward your purpose when you're willing to surrender, trust the process, and take the leap of faith. I would soon find out -the hard way- that transition isn't always pretty. In fact, it can get pretty, ugly.

My transition to my journey as CEO began with a double blow that nearly knocked me off my feet. Within the span of 30 days during the height of the COVID-19 Pandemic, in March 2020, I suddenly lost both my mother and my sister. My mom passed away from congestive heart failure, and my sister died from a stroke. The pain of suddenly losing two of the most instrumental and influential women in my life nearly cost me my own.

The immediate finality of their existence in my life felt like falling into a deep, bottomless pit. Sure, I was still alive, but a part of me died with them. I didn't know it back then, but it was a part of me that I needed to release. Losing them finally gave me the strength I had been praying for all along. My fear was gone. The part of me that was too afraid to speak my mind, to tell the truth for fear of what others might say or think about me, had vanished. The people-pleasing Stephanie no longer existed. Witnessing their quiet strength and resilience as life left their bodies transformed me. It gave birth to a new version of me, unapologetically unafraid of being brutally honest with myself and those around me about what I felt was right, was just, and what God was calling me to do and become. No longer having my mom and big sister to rely on, I was fully exposed, and fear was no longer an option.

I felt the ground transforming beneath my feet. A new journey was on the horizon, and I was ready. It's funny: When you finally let go of fear to pursue your God-given purpose, you relinquish the egoic state of being, which is all twisted up in the need for external validation. Although I didn't know my next steps, I knew clearly that life had been preparing me for this moment, and without hesitation or reservation, I stepped into the shoes God was calling me to walk in. Regardless of the cost or what I lost, I was unapologetically ready to devote the rest of my life to fulfilling my God-given purpose. I was ready to put in the work and change anything and everything that didn't serve me on my path forward. I was ready to realign.

Realigning

Whether you are in the process of realigning your career, like I was, pursuing a new role within your company, or starting a side business to increase your sources of income, you must be prepared to embrace the wait, the time between when you decide to act and when you are ready to assume your new position in life. I believe realigning toward your purpose requires four essential things:

1. The Ability to say "No"
2. Time to unplug in silence to replenish
3. Discipline
4. Patience

Every new season comes with shedding things that no longer serve you. It's something nature has been teaching us our entire lives. Yet, as we grow older, we forget and resist the beauty and peace that comes with letting go. You don't need a citation to prove this is a fact. Just think about anything new and significant in your life, whether a new birthday, school, job, or partner; every new season requires saying goodbye to something or some things. When a new season is upon us, we must graciously give ourselves time to unplug and reflect on all the areas of our lives that need change before we are prepared to move forward. Creating a visual roadmap that outlines the steps you need to take, small or big, to get you where you want to will be a great guide and help save you a whole lot of mishaps.

I wouldn't advise anyone to walk into a new season without first putting in the work necessary to ensure you will succeed. It won't be easy but remember, easy isn't how God prepares us for a life of victory. It's through trial and error that we learn, grow, and blossom into the best versions of ourselves. You didn't become an adult overnight. You didn't get to where you are now overnight, and you won't step into your vision overnight.

Effective realignment requires discipline and patience. You will pray, listen, try, and fail, and then you will pray, listen, try, and fail over and over until you eventually master the internal traits that will serve you well in your new season. Once you are fully confident that you are ready, then it's time to act.

Action

It can take anywhere from 18 to 254 days to form a new habit, with an average of 66 days for a new behavior to become automatic. It's important to know that you will not be successful in your pursuits if you try to master multiple new healthy habits simultaneously. Once you put together a list of habitual traits you want to master, whether 3, 5, 10, or 14 for me, it was around 12. You need to write down a plan detailing how you will focus on mastering every single habit. I tackled one habit from my list weekly for 12 weeks and repeated the process every 12 weeks for an entire year. I began doing this in my last corporate role. I was fully committed and promised myself that I would never make another major life move until I knew I was ready. I cannot underscore how vital mastery is. You aren't ready to pursue your dream if you cannot discipline yourself to complete a task without cheating. If you move too fast and fail to master the traits needed to elevate to the next level, you will get exposed to unfavorable elements too soon. And that early exposure could cost you your entire dream altogether. It's like seeing your child walking around in your adult-size shoes, pretending to be you, but clearly, the shoes are too big for them to fill just yet.

Only you will know when you are ready; if not, WAIT. Let the opportunity that comes along when you are still training go. The right chance won't pass you by. You will know when the time is right because you won't feel a shred of anxiety or fear. It will be your moment, transformational for you and everyone connected to you. You will move into your new season knowing that you earned it and all the new nourishment it brings to your soul.

Nourish

There is nothing like walking in nature and savoring its extraordinary beauty. It nourishes you in a way unlike anything else. It is a reminder that something greater exists beyond what you can comprehend. God wants you to savor all the blessings that come with arriving at your destination. It doesn't mean letting go of the discipline and hard work it took to achieve your dreams, but it does mean giving yourself permission to be still enough to soak in every moment of joy and wonder your new season brings. We often spend so much time rushing from one point to the next that we rush through embracing our wins like we try to rush through embracing our wait. Taking time to nourish yourself will refuel your inner strength. The sacred light you carry is unique and requires stillness to illuminate who you are entirely. Pouring into yourself will give you longevity so those connected to you can benefit from your flame as long as possible. You didn't come this far to allow the glory to burn you out.

Remember your training; keep saying "no" when you need to, unplug when you need to, stay disciplined, and set the pace. You don't have anything to prove. Fulfillment at this stage comes from a higher source. Treasure that, and keep nourishing your will to endure. Your tribe will grow, and God will ensure you have everything you need in this space to thrive. When you realize who you are. When you discover that you were born with greatness within you and that you alone have the power to hold onto it or nurture, grow, and ultimately relinquish it to the world, you have evolved.

Evolution

True evolution happens when you find balance. Your internal core values are fully aligned with your external actions. You are no longer split, having to be one person at work or in public and another in your personal environment. Your core values transcend any role, whether you are a CEO, Executive Leader, Wife, Mother, or Community Leader. You should lead with your values in every facet of your life. So, if you are bold, passionate, detailed, etc., these are traits that anyone you encounter should be able to name about you quickly. Because it is you authentically, it is the essence of who you are and should never change.

People often fearlessly defend their personal traits in their private lives but are afraid to do so publicly, so they become people-pleasers by default. When you choose to let go of the fear of being who you truly are, it means living and standing up for your values, come what may. This may mean refusing to remain in situations, friendships, or environments that don't honor your core values. Because if they don't honor your values, they don't honor you. It really is that simple.

There is something truly remarkable about an evolved woman. You can feel her essence when she speaks or steps into any room. I guess that's why I am such a major fan of Author, Spiritual Leader, and Motivational Speaker Sarah Jakes Roberts. Her personal story of evolution is exquisite. God knows she understood her assignment. As the founder of Woman Evolve, she has shared the testimony of her evolution with countless women all over the world, reminding them that the journey to becoming is as beautiful as the arrival at your destination if you allow it to be. The truth is you don't need all of the answers right away. The trials of life teach us how to stand up.

You truly do get out of life what you put into it. Healing, growth, love, success, none of it is accidental. It's earned step-by-step. If you want more, if you want to evolve, you must let go of any excuses. You can't bypass the work to get to the front of the line. If you do, it won't be fulfilling because you will know deep down that you didn't earn it. Hoping and wishing is for gamblers. The life you want doesn't come from luck; it comes from showing up day after day, no matter how hard it gets. The life you want comes with facing yourself, your fears, and your failures head-on. It comes from committing to breaking toxic cycles and patterns for good so that you experience the freedom of transformation.

Personal evolution is inner strength, clarity of mind, wisdom, balance, and unshakable peace. These traits are the true rewards you achieve when your effort and intention finally align. You will come to realize, if you haven't already, that every act of faith, discipline, prayer, and devotion to integrity when you could have taken an easier path is creating "you," the masterpiece for all the world to see. The version of you that once existed only in your dreams was always there, waiting just beneath the surface for you to unleash her, to see and love her enough to evolve into her fully. When you pour your whole heart into you, it overflows with enough love to transform your family, community, nation, and the world. That's the time for full exposure.

Exposure

You're ready for exposure when your metamorphosis is complete. When you've dared to trailblaze paths few have dared to travel. You will know the world is ready for your debut when you've crossed a great chasm. You have evolved into a love that makes you overflow with bliss, and you can't hide it even if you tried it. In this season, going backward isn't an option. You've arrived at your destiny on a firm foundation and are fully equipped to go through any storm or exposure to the elements life may bring. Your divinity at this stage is powerful. The rich can't buy it, temptation can lure it, the impatient can't rush it, and no one can steal it.

You are ready to make a difference beyond yourself. You're ready to teach what you have learned to others so they, too, can experience the beauty of divinity here on earth and pass this same treasure along to their loved ones, and so on it goes. My mom carried me in love until I was ready to be born. She watched over me until I mastered the art of love. When she died, I thought I was lost, only to realize that her love could only take me so far. All along, she was teaching me how to tap into the unique gifts God gave me. Her pearls of wisdom were the treasures she passed on to me: My love of reading, my joy of writing, and the gift to translate the light I carry into written prose. I wanted to keep my gems hidden, protected from exposure to such a harsh world. A world that trounces upon the vulnerable like wolves. But I dared to expose my gifts anyway. I dared to let go of fear. I dared to do the work with unshakable conviction and a quiet commitment to excellence. And I learned every bit of pain I experienced that felt like it was breaking me was actually building me and would eventually set me free. As Audre Lorde put it, "When I dare to be powerful, to use my strength in the service of my vision, then it becomes less & less important whether I am afraid."

I didn't set out to become the CEO of a company; I set out to become the image of me I saw in my dreams. She was brilliant, peaceable, kind, generous, healthy, and filled with abundant light, integrity, and LOVE. These characteristics transcend any title the world could ever give me. They are the jewels I pass on to my daughter, as my mom and sister passed on to me. I was ready for exposure when I let go of being a people-pleasing imposter hiding beneath titles the world gave me and just became me, the soul God created me to be…fully and free.

Here are 4 Challenges I Want to Leave With You:

1. Get still enough to really find out your WHY. If you aren't completely sure you are on the right path, stop walking. Imagine you're climbing a mountain. Without knowing what's at the top, would you keep going? You'll never reach your destination going the wrong way.
2. Change your internal dialogue. Instead of "I hope I can do this." Say, "I can do this. Instead of saying, "It's too hard for me." Say, "This challenge I'll learn from." Instead of saying, "I'm stuck." Say, "This situation is making me stronger to move forward." Instead of saying, "If I stop, I'm done." Say, "It's okay to take a break and return stronger."
3. Commit to mastering the art of discipline. Discipline really isn't about forcing yourself to work or do anything. True discipline is creating an environment where the work you need to do feels natural; your mindset is such that setbacks are simply lessons, and your vision is so clear that you are compelled to keep moving forward, come what may, because you refuse

to stop until you finish the masterpiece in the making that is YOU.
4. Let go of fear and embrace the wait. Timing is everything!

When it's your time to shine, nothing will dim your light or extinguish your flame.

About the Author
Stephanie Johnson

Award Winning Journalist | Marketing | Public Relations | Communications Consultant

An Emmy award-winning journalist, author and communications thought leader with more than two decades of media-integrated marketing, public relations, and crisis communications expertise, Stephanie (Steph) Johnson is the CEO & Founder of BrandDNA Group, a Public Relations (PR) and Communications consultancy that specializes in serving brands driving innovation for the good of humanity.

Steph has a proven track record of creating and delivering compelling stories and messages to advance the mission and vision of the brands she serves. During her tenure as Senior Vice President of Enterprise

Communications at the American Cancer Society (ACS), Steph helped to re-imagine ACS's strategic blueprint for internal and external communications, executive thought leadership, and crisis/issues management response. Prior to her role at ACS, Steph spent a year expanding her expertise on a Global scale at Hotwire Global, an International Public Relations Agency. As a Global VP and Communications Strategist, she helped create executive thought leadership platforms and strategic communications road maps for some of the world's leading Tech brands.

Before branching out to expand her expertise with in-house PR agency experience, Steph spent nearly a decade as VP of Communications & Product Strategies at the American Medical Association (AMA). Prior to her role at the AMA, Steph served as VP of Public Affairs at Advocate Aurora Health. As a journalist for 7+ years, Steph got her start in television, working for ABC News Good Morning America and World News Tonight with Peter Jennings. She also worked as a freelance producer for the Chicago Bureaus of ABC & NBC News, as a TV news anchor for 16 WAPT News, the ABC News Affiliate in her home state of Mississippi. Steph graduated Summa Com Laude with a Bachelor of Science in Broadcast Journalism and a minor in Speech and Dramatic Arts.

Contact Information:
BrandDNA Group
Website: www.branddnagroup.com
LinkedIn: http://linkedin.com/in/stepjohnson

Conclusion

The Call to Redefine Leadership; Together

Shayla N. Atkins

Leadership is at a crossroads.

For too long, we have operated within a leadership model that prioritized authority over authenticity, visibility over value, and command over collaboration. Traditional leadership paradigms, rooted in rigid hierarchies and outdated performance measures, no longer meet the demands of today's dynamic, diverse, and innovation driven workplaces.

Yet, despite clear evidence that human-centered leadership drives performance, engagement, and profitability, many organizations still resist evolving their leadership standards.

The question is no longer *whether* leadership must change, but who will change it, and the answer is us.

If you've read this far, then you are already a part of the movement. This book was never meant to be the final word, it is the *beginning* of a larger conversation. A conversation about what leadership should be, how it should serve, and how it should evolve.

Leadership Is More Than a Title; It's a Responsibility

Research shows that poor leadership costs U.S. companies an estimated $630 billion annually due to disengagement, turnover, and lost productivity (Gallup, 2023). Meanwhile, organizations that prioritize trust, purpose, and inclusion outperform their competitors in innovation, collaboration, and long-term profitability (McKinsey, 2022).

This is why the leadership standard must change, not just for ourselves but also for the businesses, employees, and industries we influence.

The future of leadership does not belong to those who manage through power and position, it belongs to those who lead through purpose and impact.

Leaders must master the human dimensions of leadership to lead people, develop, inspire, and elevate them.

The Essential Human Leadership Skills: They Are No Longer "Soft" Skills

For decades, skills like empathy, emotional intelligence, purpose-driven leadership, and communication have been dismissed as *soft*, secondary to technical business skills.

The question is, are we managing work and robots, or are we leading people, leading humans?

But here's the reality:

- 90% of top-performing leaders possess high emotional intelligence, which correlates with 58% of job performance success (Goleman, 2020).
- Leaders who demonstrate empathy increase team engagement, innovation, and performance (Gentry et

al., 2016).
- Organizations that foster psychological safety, where employees feel safe to contribute ideas, outperform others in creativity, problem-solving, and team effectiveness (Edmondson, 2019).
- Employees who see their work as meaningful are 3x more likely to stay with their organization and are 125% more productive (McKinsey, 2022).

If the ability to lead, inspire, and drive results depends on empathy, trust, communication, and strategic thinking, then these are not soft skills, they are essential leadership skills.

They should be the standard.

Will You Accept the Call?

This book was never about simply reading leadership strategies, it was about deciding what kind of leader you will be.

So, I ask you:

- How will you redefine leadership in your sphere of influence?
- What outdated leadership beliefs are you ready to leave behind?
- How will you ensure your leadership reflects both authenticity and impact?

- What conversations will you start that challenge the status quo?

This is your moment. This is your movement.

Lead boldly. Lead authentically. Lead Strategically, Together. Lead with S.P.I.C.E.®

"The next era of leadership is already being built. The only question is: Will you lead it?"

Thank you for reading our stories, strategies, trials and triumphs. We hope you find this book to be a compass, a roadmap, a guide to take action and accelerate your leadership journey.

Stay positive. Lead with Love, Light and Humanity.

Sources

McKinsey & Company, & LeanIn.Org. (2019). Women in the workplace 2019. McKinsey & Company. https://www.mckinsey.com/~/media/McKinsey/Featured%20Insights/Gender%20Equality/Women%20in%20the%20Workplace%202019/Women-in-the-workplace-2019.pdf

Buckingham, M., & Goodall, A. (2022).
Love + Work: How to find what you love, love what you do, and do it for the rest of your life. Harvard Business Review Press.

Businessolver. (2022).
2022 State of Workplace Empathy Report.
https://www.businessolver.com/

Covey, S. R. (1989).
The 7 habits of highly effective people: powerful lessons in personal change. Free Press.

DiSC. (n.d.).
DiSC model overview. https://www.discprofile.com/what-is-disc/overview

Drucker, P. F. (1974).
Management: tasks, responsibilities, practices. Harper & Row.

Dweck, C. S. (2006).
Mindset: The new psychology of success. Random House.

Development Dimensions International. (2023).
Leadership effectiveness through 360-degree feedback [research report]. Pittsburgh, PA: DDI.

Elsesser, K. (2024, June 5).

Female CEOs outearn male counterparts in S&P 500 companies. Forbes. https://www.forbes.com/sites/kimelsesser/2024/06/05/female-ceos-outearn-male-counterparts-in-sp-500-companies/

Gallup. (2024). *State of the global workplace 2024 report.* https://www.gallup.com/workplace/349484/state-of-the-global-workplace.aspx

Joy of Performing. (2025). When managers apply the continuous feedback loop. Retrieved January 10, 2025, from https://www.getjop.com/blog/when-managers-apply-the-continuous-feedback-loop

Robbins, T. (n.d.). [Quote about business as a spiritual game]. https://www.tonyrobbins.com

Society for Human Resource Management. (2024). Impact of 360-degree feedback on organizational performance [research report]. SHRM.

Adult Children of Alcoholics by Janet G. Woititz
Woititz, J. G. (1983). *Adult Children of Alcoholics*. Health Communications, Inc.

The Coaching Habit: Say Less, Ask More & Change the Way You Lead Forever
Bungay Stanier, M. (2016). *The Coaching Habit: Say Less, Ask More & Change the Way You Lead Forever*. Box of Crayons Press.

Catalyst. (2023). Quick take: Women in the workforce—United States and Canada. Retrieved from https://www.catalyst.org/research/women-in-the-workforce-united-states-and-canada/

McKinsey & Company. (2022). Women in the workplace 2022. Retrieved from https://www.mckinsey.com/featured-insights/diversity-and-inclusion/women-in-the-workplace

Pew Research Center. (2018). Views on leadership traits and perceptions of male and female leaders. Retrieved from (https://www.pewresearch.org/](https://www.pewresearch.org/)

Zenger, J., & Folkman, J. (2019, June 25). Research: Women are better leaders during a crisis. Harvard Business Review. Retrieved from https://hbr.org/2019/06/research-women-are-better-leaders-in-a-crisis

Center for Talent Innovation. (2019). Being black in corporate America: An intersectional exploration. Retrieved from https://coqual.org/

Christine L Exley, Judd B Kessler (2022). The Gender Gap in Self-Promotion. The Quarterly Journal of Economics, 137(3), 1345–1381. https://doi.org/10.1093/qje/qjac003

Internet / Online Source: www.natcom.org /about-nca/what-communication.

Gallup, *State of the American Manager: Analytics and Advice for Leaders*, Gallup Press, 2015.